LORD OF ALL LIFE

LoRD of all LIFE

A. IAN BURNETT, M.A., D.D.

Minister of St. Andrew's
Presbyterian Church, Ottawa

New York
RINEHART & CO. INC.

To
THE MEMORY OF
MY FATHER

ALEXANDER BURNETT

whose joy it was to serve
The Lord Of All Life as
Man and Missionary all
the days of his life.

"He walked before the Lord in truth and with a perfect heart".
II KINGS 20:3.

ACKNOWLEDGEMENTS

In PREPARING these pages, I have tried to verify and acknowledge every reference and quotation. If I have in any instance failed to do so, it has been because the original source has completely escaped me, and I crave the indulgence of any whom I may have thus offended.

I wish to acknowledge the kindness shown to me by Mr. R. W. W. Robertson, of Messrs. Clarke, Irwin & Company who has done so much to see this book through the press; and last but certainly not least the unfailing encouragement and ungrudging assistance given me by my wife through all the years.

PREFACE

ST. PAUL has told us that his guiding principle in all preaching was to make known "Jesus Christ and Him crucified". Down the centuries the Christian Church has known that it possesses no other Gospel. Where Christ has been held high, the Church has marched forward to new conquests: where men have departed from this central truth it has faltered and failed. The promise, "I, if I be lifted up, will draw all men unto me", remains true for every age, and this atomic age is no exception.

During the past twenty-one years, it has been my greatest privilege to preach Christ as the Lord of all life on both sides of the Atlantic. The present volume contains a selection from that preaching. The first three groups of addresses were delivered as series of sermons to my people in St. Andrew's Church, Ottawa, whose loyalty and appreciation have been a constant inspiration to their minister. Of the remainder, some were preached many years ago to the gallant fisherfolk of the Scottish village of Newhaven, and others to the wartime toilers in the great railway centre of Springburn in the City of Glasgow.

This one thing, however, the years have taught me. This Gospel, which however falteringly and inadequately I have tried to declare week by week, is the one Gospel for all men,—the only Gospel for our World. It met the needs of fishermen risking their lives in the little boats that battled against the long swell which runs across the fishing banks of the North Sea. It brought comfort and courage, hope and peace to men labouring in great modern soulless factories or squaring their shoulders to meet the shocks and sorrows of war. It is the Gospel too which has brought grace and strength, resolution and courage to those who know something of "the lonely greatness of the world". It is the Gospel for prince and statesman, for the senate and the marketplace, for the study and the home. Jesus Christ remains the Lord of all life.

A. Ian Burnett

Ash Wednesday
1952

CONTENTS

BEHOLD THE MAN

I

"EMMANUEL — GOD WITH US"

Behold, a virgin shall be with child, and shall bring
forth a son, and they shall call his name EMMANUEL,
which being interpreted is, GOD WITH US.

ST. MATTHEW 1:23.

ON THAT first Christmas Eve, over nineteen centuries
ago, a loiterer in the inn courtyard at Bethlehem might
have had his attention arrested by the sight of a weary,
anxious man leading a small donkey on which sat a
young peasant woman obviously on the verge of
collapse. Across the sunlit courtyard they passed,
slowly and softly, to be lost from sight through the
darkness of the stable door beyond. Few, if any, of
the large crowd thronging the Bethlehem streets that
afternoon were interested enough to notice the arrival
of that pathetic little group, and not until some hours
later did the guests in the inn hear the news that a
baby boy had been born that evening without in the
stable. No doubt there were those of the company
who expressed sympathy for the young mother in her
plight, but soon the little drama would be forgotten
in the interest of some new topic of conversation.

Of one thing we can be quite certain. Not one
person who heard of the birth of that babe ever associated him with the Child of Isaiah's prophecy. To
have suggested that it was the Messiah who was lying
asleep out there in the manger would have been to
court the ridicule of all who heard. To have claimed
that this child was none other than God Incarnate,

3

"God with us", would have been regarded as blasphemy and might well have ended with the blasphemer being stoned out of Bethlehem.

Yet, in the birth of that babe so long ago, not only have we the explanation of the persistence of the Christian Church, but we have also the one great reason for the universal busyness of Christmastide—for the buying and selling, the revelling and rejoicing, the exultant happiness of our children and the general spirit of goodwill pervading the world at this season of the year. Christmas comes and once more hearts are glad; homes are radiant.

> Blow, bugles of battle, the marches of peace;
> East, west, north and south let the long quarrel cease;
> Sing the song of great joy that the angels began,
> Sing the glory of God and of good-will to man!
> Sing the glory of God and of good-will to man![1]

Now why should the birth of that child mean the inflow of so much joy and gladness into the midst of dull, winter days? Why these parties and presents? Why this universal atmosphere of goodwill penetrating even to the office and workshop and market place?

St. Matthew, searching the Old Testament for references to Christ, found the final answer to these questions in Isaiah's famous prophecy: "Behold, a virgin shall be with child, and shall bring forth a son, and they shall call his name Emmanuel, which being interpreted is, God with us". That beautiful Hebrew word "Emmanuel" is the key to an understanding of the whole spirit and message of Christmas. Christmas

----

[1] J. G. Whittier, *A Christmas Carmen.*

stands for this, is remembered for this,—that God came down at Christmastide.

Let us consider, then, how it was that God came down that first Christmas Day and in what sense the birth of Jesus may be interpreted as "God with us".

"They shall call his name Emmanuel, God with us". In the first place, Christmas reminds us that we are inhabitants of a world in which Jesus has actually lived. He was really born in Bethlehem of Judea. The cradle and the babe, the wise men and the shepherds, the angels and the star, are not just fragments of a beautiful dream, but solid historical facts. Men have seen Christ face to face. They have listened to Him teaching, have watched Him working, have touched Him with their hands, have witnessed Him die and rise again. Jesus Christ was a real man. His life is a fact of world history.

I can never forget how intense this sense of the reality of Jesus became as we travelled through Palestine a few years ago. How wonderful to stand on the very floor of the synagogue in Capernaum where His feet once rested! How moving to go down to the edge of the Sea of Galilee at midnight with the moon making a silver pathway over the waters and know that one dark night He walked those self-same waters! Or imagine standing in that cave in Bethlehem which was once a stable and knowing that here within these very walls He was born! Galilee and Nazareth, Bethlehem and Jerusalem, they are real places, sacred today because Jesus lived and walked in them. He is real, this Christ "who was born of the Virgin Mary, suffered under Pontius Pilate, was crucified, dead and buried,— the third day He rose again from the dead". That is the historic truth about Him, indisputable, unassailable.

Yet there is more behind that fact than we may casually imagine. The fact that Christ has actually been born and has lived in this world is nothing less than a revelation of the Creator of the world Himself. It tells us that the God who created this Universe is the kind of God who was able to give us Jesus Christ. And because I find it impossible to believe, as does the atheist or the naturalist that the creature can ever be greater than his Creator, I must, therefore, believe that God in Heaven is at least as good and loving, as merciful and compassionate as was Jesus Christ.

Had Handel been born deaf and throughout his life never heard one note of music, could we ever have been thrilled by the magnificent glory of the Hallelujah Chorus? Had Caruso been dumb how could we have listened spellbound to the music of that superb tenor voice? If Robert Burns had been born blind, could he ever have sung so sweetly of the bonny banks and braes of Ayrshire or painted with such perfect artistry of words the beauties of his native land? Of course not! Without the powers of hearing, of speech, of sight, these things could not have been. And neither could this world have known Christ Jesus, unless over and around it is a God as gracious and good, as loving and self-sacrificing as the Lord Himself.

The fact of Christ, writes Dr. Carnegie Simpson, "does not indeed show us everything, but it shows us the one thing we need to know—the character of God. God is the God who sent Jesus."[1] In other words, God must be like Christ. The character of the Creator

[1] P. Carnegie Simpson, *The Fact of Christ*. Hodder & Stoughton Ltd.

cannot be less than the highest He has created, and the highest is that babe born to Mary on that first Christmas morning.

No wonder then, Christmas is such a time of joy, for Christmas means that God is with us in Christ; that He is Christlike; that we live in a world governed and controlled by the Lord of Love, the Father of our Lord Jesus Christ. Remember that when dark clouds of worry and fear threaten to hide the sun for you. Remember it when temptations and sins threaten your soul with disaster. "Where sin abounds, grace doth much more abound."[1] A Christlike God is upon the throne of this universe.

There is another sense, however, in which the birth of Jesus means that God is with us. Frequently we speak of someone being "with us", when we really mean that we have their sympathy, their understanding, their support. And Christmas tells us that God is with us in sympathy and understanding, for through Christ He has had a share in our mortal life. "God was in Christ." That has always been the Christian faith about the man, Christ Jesus. Mary's babe is none other than the only begotten Son of God, very God of very God. And what Jesus has experienced, God has also experienced.

Let us go then to Bethlehem and watch Mary bending over her child. This infant asleep in her arms is none other than the mighty God Himself, and yet how utterly dependent He is upon His mother's love and His father's care! Like any other child, He has to be suckled and nursed, crooned to sleep and comforted when He cries.

[1] Romans 5:20.

Who ran to help Him when He fell,
And would some pretty story tell,
Or kiss the place to make it well?
    His Mother.

Cross the hills to Nazareth and watch the child Jesus
grow from boyhood to manhood. See Him sitting with
the other boys of the village in the old Rabbi's class-
room at the synagogue spelling out his first letters.
Listen to Him at His mother's knee lisping His first
childish prayer. Stand there in the carpenter's shop
and watch while Joseph gives Him the first lesson of
His apprenticeship. So the years passed and swiftly
the responsibilities of manhood came upon Him. There
were days when He shared the anxieties of His parents
over their daily bread. There were long nights when
He helped to watch by a brother's or sister's sick bed.
Yes, and there was that sad day when He was one of
the little company who laid Joseph to rest in God's
Acre on the hill above Nazareth. And so we could
pass in review the whole of His life, finding at every
point experiences common to all. Jesus lived a human
life. He lived, indeed, the kind of life which is common
to all men.

You recall how the writer to the Hebrews was
thrilled by this thought of God in Christ sharing the
joys and sorrows, the difficulties and hardships which
are our daily companions. Writing to his fellow Christians who were passing through the fires of persecution,
he reminds them that "we have not a High Priest that
cannot be touched with the feeling of our infirmities;
but one that hath been in all points tempted (or tried)
like as we are, yet without sin. Let us therefore," he
goes on, "draw near with boldness unto the throne of

grace, that we may receive mercy, and find grace to help in time of need."[1]

"I have often observed," writes Mark Rutherford, "that the greatest help we get in time of trouble comes to us from some friend who says quite simply, 'I have endured all that'." And that is precisely what God says to us. Through Christ He has endured all that we have to endure. He has experienced what life is like. He knows it from the inside. The result is that He is able to help us for He understands the "feeling of our infirmities".

Christmas speaks to us all of this, for Christmas marks the beginning of God sharing in human experience. "And his name shall be called Emmanuel, God with us"—God with us in sympathy, in understanding, in love. Let the thought that He knows be our comfort and strength this Christmas. He knows!

> Partaker of the human name,
> He knows the frailty of our frame.
>
> In every pang that rends the heart,
> The Man of Sorrows had a part;
> He sympathizes with our grief,
> And to the sufferer sends relief.[2]

No wonder we rejoice at Christmas when God is with us in so wonderful a way!

The greatest of all reasons for our Christmas joy and Christmas hope, however, is just this: that God is still with us. He is with us in person, the Partner of

[1] Hebrews 4: 15-16. (R.V.)

[2] Scottish Paraphrases: "Where high the heav'nly temple stands" No. 58.

our lives, the Friend of our souls, the Guide for our future, the Lord of everlasting glory. Matthew begins his Gospel by quoting Isaiah's glorious prophecy: "They shall call his name Emmanuel, God with us." He closes it by quoting that still more glorious promise made by the triumphant Lord Himself: "Lo, I am with you alway, even unto the end of the world."[1] God is with us still for Christ Jesus is with us alway.

The birth of Mary's babe in Bethlehem would not of itself have been sufficient to account for our presence within our Churches 1900 years after the event; nor could it alone explain the world-wide joy of the Christmas season. We rejoice today not just because Jesus lived: we rejoice because *He lives*. He is the same today as yesterday,—the same wonderful Friend and Saviour, the same mighty Lord and Master, the same immortal Son of God. And Christmas is remembered the world over with so much gladness and goodwill because it marks the beginning of this amazing, transforming friendship between men and the Saviour of men,—a friendship as real and accessible today as it was two thousand years ago.

Jesus Christ is still the living Comrade of countless lives. That is the Christmas message *par excellence*. Tens of thousands today know Him like that, a living Presence in their lives, an unseen Friend by their side, an Immortal Lover who will not let them go. Indeed, it is only when by faith and prayer we know Jesus in this vital way, that our religion becomes a real, a living, an unconquerable faith.

Dr. Leslie Weatherhead, the minister of the City Temple, tells how once he attended an interesting pro-

[1] St. Matthew 28: 20.

gramme of illusions in London. One of the items was called "The Artist's Dream". The artist had fallen asleep near an almost completed portait of his wife who had just died. The picture showed her sitting on a swing in a garden. As the artist slept, the woman in the picture stepped down from the easel and walked across the studio to where her husband slept. Behind her you could see the empty swing. Then she returned, and the artist wakened. The dream had been so real that he walked over to the easel and taking down the picture, examined it in front of the audience. But apparently it was just an ordinary picture.[1]

Multitudes today are worshipping a picture of Jesus in a frame called "history". They are looking back wistfully and sadly towards Bethlehem, regretting that they cannot take to Him their gifts of gold and frankincense and myrrh, while the struggle to be like their Hero and Ideal humbles and humiliates them. How much such people need to be told that a richer and more wonderful experience than ever they have imagined possible can be theirs, and theirs today! Only let them sit down quietly and give faith and love for Christ their way, and the Son of Mary, Jesus of Nazareth, will come down out of the picture of history and memory and imagination in which we have framed Him. He will step right into our lives, the most real of all real beings, the ever-living, ever-loving Lord and Companion of our days, the Friend above all others who will never leave nor forsake us. For He whom prophets foretold and angels proclaimed is still "Emmanuel—God with us" reconciling the world unto Himself.

[1] Leslie Weatherhead, *The Transforming Friendship*. The Epworth Press.

II

HIS FEET

And He said unto them . . . Behold . . . my feet, that
it is I myself . . . And He shewed them . . . His feet.
St. Luke 24:38-40.

IF ONE were asked to pick out the one outstanding
characteristic which distinguished the feet of our Lord
from any other feet that have ever trod this earth, my
choice would fall on their far-travelledness. How far-
travelled they were! Once they were tiny baby feet,
which Mary, His mother, could all-enclose in one of
her own small hands. Once they were little, elfish feet
which Joseph so loved to tease and torment as He lay
laughing in His cradle. On the warm, soft sands of
Egypt, where Moses had played as a boy, they first
learned the high art of walking, and there Mary caught
her first glimpse of the ominous shadow of the Cross
as her first-born Son stumbled towards her with arms
outstretched and the streaming light behind Him cast
that dark, dread shadow twixt her and Him.

Later, those feet roamed the highlands of Galilee;
explored the deep corries and towering chimneys
around Mount Carmel; carried Him to school and
synagogue, to well and workshop and village store.
Later still, they supported Him through long hot days
as He toiled at the carpenter's bench,—sawing, plan-
ing, measuring, hammering, fitting and fashioning all
the multitude of furnishings required for the homes
and homesteads of Nazareth. Those baby feet Mary
had so tenderly wrapped in swaddling clothes had

12

grown to man's estate; had grown sure, steady, strong as a rock. Shod simply in sandals, sandals which are so easily slipped off for worship and on for service, they carried Him to the very end of the road without fail or falter.

From the Gospels we know how hard He used those feet of His and how far He drove them. From Nazareth to Jordan, from Jordan out to the burning, stony wilderness and back to Galilee, they carried Him. Through countless city streets and village roads by day, and far into lonely, silent places among the hills by night, they bore Him. They took Him up the slopes of Mount Hermon to where the snows lay deep, and down to the hot, sultry plains around Jericho. They brought Him along "The Way of Blood" to Jerusalem, and each night of that last fateful week back to the quiet of Bethany. Those feet His disciples followed through the sleeping, silent streets of the Holy City to an Upper Room, and later to a Garden, and beyond to Judgment and the Cross. Those feet Roman soldiers held in their vice and pinioned with great nails to the wood of the Cross, so that forevermore they bear the print of the nails, the stigmata, the sign and seal of our Saviour and Redeemer.

In very truth, they were far-travelled those feet of Jesus, far-travelled despite the fact that they hardly ever carried Him beyond the narrow frontiers of His own small land of Palestine. They took Him from Bethlehem to Calvary, but in doing so they carried Him so much further than even we can ever realize. For there is a real sense, the most real of all, in which they brought Him from heaven to earth, from earth to hell, and back to heaven again. Those feet of Jesus carried Him across the frontiers of all mortal experience and immortal agonies: make no mistake of that! They took Mary's Child and made Him the Lord and Master, the Saviour and Redeemer of men, "the Lamb of God which taketh away the sin of the World".[1] We dare not forget how far-travelled they were, and we do well to mark the way they went!

One obvious truth emerges from this consideration. Glibly, thoughtlessly, foolishly, we often speak of following in the footsteps of Christ. Yet how little any of us know of all that means! Certainly, in one sense, we can never follow where He has trod. We cannot travel from Bethlehem to Calvary on the spiritual pilgrimage which He undertook. Thank God there is no need for any of us to make that forlorn attempt, for it was for our sakes and for our salvation that Christ, the Lord, took this road, and bore our own sins in His body, and purchased forever our eternal redemption. Only God could do this for us. Only God in Christ could reconcile the world unto Himself.

But none of the ransomed ever knew,
   How deep were the waters crossed,
Nor how dark was the night that the Lord passed through,
   Ere He found His sheep that was lost.[2]

Without doubt there is one sense in which we can never follow in His footsteps, even if we would!

But He did not fail us. His feet did not fail us, for He travelled the road to its bitter end, to Gethsemane and Golgotha and the Grave. Other feet have sometimes failed on other ways. It was largely due to the failure of their feet that Scott and his party perished

---

[1] St. John 1:29.
[2] Elizabeth Cecilia Clephane, "There were ninety and nine".

on that tragic journey back from the South Pole. Captain Oates was the first to disclose his badly, frost-bitten feet. "Poor Oates," wrote Scott in his journal on the second of March, "is unable to pull, sits on the sledge when we are search-tracking—he is wonderfully plucky as his feet must be giving him great pain." Two days later Edward Wilson's feet began troubling him "mainly because he gives so much help to others," added Scott. A week and a day later Oates made the heroic sacrifice of himself in the hope of saving his companions, but by then it was too late. Their feet failed them. "We have decided to die naturally in the track," wrote Scott in that last, unforgettable message to the public.[1] Their feet gave out, and they did not get through.

But not so the feet of Him who took the hardest, longest, darkest road in human history! His feet carried Him through to the end. On the last bleak mile they stumbled a little as He dragged the wood of the Cross up the hill called Calvary. But they brought Him there at the last, and made Him our everlasting Saviour and Redeemer and Lord.

A further thought suggests itself. If those feet of His did not fail Him, if, indeed, they carried Him through to triumphant and eternal victory, do some of us still cling to the foolish illusion that they will now fail Him, now that He is the Lord of Glory? Or even more foolishly, do we imagine that we can escape those feet? Do we think the Christ cannot find us, will not find us, hunt us down and bring us captive into His Kingdom? There are those who cling to such follies,

[1] George Seaver, *Edward Wilson of the Antarctic*. John Murray, London.

arguing that because it is nineteen hundred years and more since He walked the earth, since men looked upon His face or heard His voice or touched His hand, therefore we can escape from Him. He cannot reach us. He will not find us. We are safe from Him! Oh, foolish heart! When will you learn that no one can escape Him, for in those three and thirty years of His earthly life He beat a path for Himself into every human heart. He made Himself Lord of all men's lives, so that today there is no escape. Sooner or later we may expect Him to surprise and challenge us, to call and command and conquer.

He is the inescapable Christ, this Jesus of Nazareth. Bar your door, lock and bolt it with every means you possess, and He will pass into the innermost sanctuary as though nothing were there. Curse Him, if you dare; turn your back upon Him; shut your eyes and stop your ears: and you will find Him as the Thought in your heart, the Image in your mind, the voiceless Voice in your soul.

Poor, rebellious, unhappy Francis Thompson thought that he at least could escape this merciless Seeker. He tells us how long and passionately he sought to outwit Him:

I fled Him, down the nights and down the days;
   I fled Him down the arches of the years;
I fled Him, down the labyrinthine ways
   Of my own mind; and in the mist of tears
I hid from Him, and under running laughter.
      Up vistaed hopes I sped;
      And shot, precipitated,
Adown Titanic glooms of chasmed fears,
   From those strong Feet, that followed, followed after.

But with unhurrying chase,
And unperturbed pace,
Deliberate speed, majestic instancy,
They beat—and a Voice beat
More instant than the Feet—
"All things betray thee, who betrayest Me."

So the chase proceeded, but in vain. Always there came behind those "following Feet", until at last:

Halts by me that footfall:
Is my gloom, after all,
Shade of His hand, outstretched caressingly?
"Ah, fondest, blindest, weakest,
I am He Whom thou seekest!
Thou dravest love from thee, who dravest Me."[1]

There lies the reason we can never escape Him. He is Love, Love Incarnate,

Love, that is first and last of all things made,
The light that has the living world for shade,
The spirit that for temporal veil has on
The souls of all men woven in unison.[2]

As well try to escape from the air we breathe, as escape this Spirit of Love abroad in the universe. Love is everywhere, and where Love is, God is, Christ is; and His footprints upon time are the imprints of a million feet busy about Love's business.

No, there is no escaping this following, seeking Christ! He finds us when we think we have escaped Him. He meets us even when we know it not, and into

---

[1] Francis Thompson, *The Hound of Heaven*. Burns, Oates & Washbourne Ltd. Courtesy Sir Francis Meynell.

[2] Algernon Charles Swinburne, "Tristram of Lyonesse".

the secret place of every human heart has beaten a
path for His own blessed feet. For—

"I am He Whom thou seekest!
Thou dravest love from thee, who dravest Me."

It follows from all this that though in one sense we
cannot follow in our Lord's footsteps, yet when He
seeks and finds us, we must obey His call which, today
as of old is the challenge: "Follow Me!" Christian
discipleship is still a matter of following in His footsteps. Moreover, because His way is ever the way of
love, the marks of His footprints are always clear
before us on the road of life.

"Love," declared St. Paul, echoing His Master, "is
the fulfilling of the law."[1] For Jesus Himself had
summed up the whole law of religion in terms of love.
"Thou shalt love the Lord thy God with all thy heart,
and with all thy soul, and with all thy strength, and
with all thy mind; and thy neighbour as thyself."[2] To
love God with every fibre of one's being and to love
others as we love ourselves—that is the heart of Christianity. Do this and we shall live. Do this and we
follow in Christ's footsteps.

To think of our faith in terms of such love is to be
brought to the supreme touchstone by which the value
of our discipleship is tested. For Jesus this love meant
two things in actual practice. On the one hand, it
meant a passionate, persistent desire to have fellowship
with God His Father, a desire so deep that He was
constantly sacrificing His own comfort and rest and
sleep in order to keep open those channels of com-

[1] Romans 13:10.
[2] St. Luke 10:27.

munion. On the other hand, it meant a prodigal
spending of Himself to save and heal, to comfort and
console, to strengthen and encourage others. Throughout His life, His own personal interests and desires and
preferences took last place. He loved God with all His
being, and He loved others before Himself.

Compare this faith on fire with love with that
quality of faith which we so often regard as adequate
for Christian discipleship, and it becomes only too
clear how far we fall short of our Lord's high purpose
for us. This coldly rational acceptance of a creed, this
merely negative morality so self-centred in its outlook,
this easy satisfaction with the lowest common denomi-
nator in conduct, is little better than a caricature of
the faith and following which our Lord expects from
us. We have believed with our minds and have followed with our reasons, but our hearts have not been
kindled. The white flame of love for God in Christ
has not welded faith into an all-embracing whole, so
that every part of our being might be brought into
harmony with the will of God. More love is what we
need, more love for God and Christ and for the brethren. Without it faith can never come alive, and our
following in the footsteps of our Lord remain no more
than a poor, lame stumbling that must forever keep us
far behind.

You remember how, after the Resurrection, our
Lord, gathered with His disciples by the shore of the
Sea of Galilee, turned to Simon Peter with the thrice-
repeated question, "Simon, son of Jonas, lovest thou
Me?" Three times Peter gave the assurance that he
did love Christ and each time Jesus concluded with the
command, "Feed my sheep!" But that was not all, for
at the very end Christ spoke to Simon and His last

word was the same as His first: "Follow Me!"[1]   There
can be no following of Christ that will last unless it is
undergirded by love for Christ.   Love is the great
alchemist that alone can transform faith into following,
make a creed into conviction, and change the stumbling instability of a Simon into the rock-like firmness
of Peter, the Apostle and Martyr. "Lovest thou Me?"
asks Jesus. If, like Peter, we can answer, "Yea, Lord,
thou knowest that I love Thee!", then we too shall
follow in His footsteps right to the very end of the road.

[1] St. John 21:15-19.

III

HIS GARMENTS

And after that they had mocked Him, they took the robe off from Him, and put His own raiment on Him, and led Him away to crucify Him.

St. Matthew 27:31.

CLOTHES, despite the fact that there are always people ready to decry their importance, have a distinctive value of their own and play a vital part in human life. For one thing they serve the very practical purpose of protecting us against the inclemency of the weather, against blazing sun or biting frost. Then again their social value is hardly to be rated too highly. Through the medium of clothes woman has constantly sought to attract and hold the interest of her male partner, while for men clothes have always provided an index of social and economic stability. So often, too, we describe a person by the clothes he wears. We speak of a man being "down-at-heel"; we talk of others as being "black-coated workers", or "brass hats", or "fashion plates". If not always true, at least on many occasions it is true that clothes provide a mirror to the character of their wearer, and a man's clothes become absorbed in his personality.

One other fact is important. Clothes are always changing. Every season brings its new fashions, and though on the surface the change may appear to be quite fortuitous, a definite plan is constantly working itself out. There is what we might call a law of fashion by which the garments of the aristocracy are constantly becoming the dress of the ordinary masses. "The nakedness of the indigent world may be clothed from the trimmings of the vain,"[1] wrote Oliver Goldsmith, and that is precisely what is always happening. The cast-offs of the rich become the everyday garb of the poor, and by means of clothes the humbler run of men are for ever striving to raise themselves up to the levels of the great and mighty.

Considering this importance of clothes, it cannot be irrelevant to spend time thinking of the part which they played in the life of our Lord. Like us, He too wore clothes. First, there was His linen shirt, over which was worn a tunic or mantle, also of white linen and woven "without seam"[2] so that it fitted closely at the neck. Round His waist was a linen girdle, and over all was drawn a loosely fitting garment of white woolen cloth decorated with tassels at the corners. On His feet were sandals, while His head would probably be covered by a white linen napkin wound round in turban fashion, with the ends falling loosely over the neck.

On numerous occasions the evangelists refer to His clothing. Mary wrapped her new-born son "in swaddling clothes and laid Him in a manger".[3] During His ministry His garb proved as potent as His person, and to touch the hem of His garment meant life and health for many a sick one. At the Transfiguration, His clothes as well as His face became radiant with glory. In the Upper Room, we read that He laid aside His outer garments and girded Himself with a towel before washing the disciples' feet. Following His trial, Roman

---

[1] Oliver Goldsmith, *The Vicar of Wakefield.*

[2] St. John 19:23.

[3] St. Luke 2:7.

soldiers clothed Him in purple and scarlet as a prelude
to their mockery of Him.   Yet when He came to die,
He went forth "in His own clothes".[1]   On Good Friday
night, Joseph of Arimathea wrapped His body in white
grave clothes, the ordinary linen shroud for the dead,
while in the Book of Revelation we read of the triumphant, glorified Lord being clothed "with a vesture
dipped in blood . . . and He hath on His vesture a
name written, King of Kings and Lord of Lords".[2]

Our Lord's clothes were important, and the use to
which He put them remains significant.   Furthermore,
reflection reveals three types of clothing which He had
to wear, and it is from this standpoint that we had
best pursue our study.

Going back to the very beginning, we must note in
the first place those clothes which He had to wear
because of His birth in our nature and His identity
with our race.   "The Word was made flesh"[3] we read,
and in consequence of that Mary "brought forth her
firstborn son, and wrapped Him in swaddling clothes".
The first clothes worn by the Incarnate Son of God
were those garments woven within the mysterious loom
of life we call the womb, clothes woven out of the
strange fabrics of flesh and blood and bone, which
afterwards His mother wrapped so tenderly in the soft
protecting folds of the swaddling clothes her fingers
had so carefully and lovingly fashioned.

Here are those garments which God chose for His
own Son, *the clothes of God's choosing*.   Here is the
dress which the Saviour of the world had no option

[1] St. Mark 15:20.
[2] Revelation 19:13, 16.
[3] St. John 1:14.

but to wear in order that He might bring many sons to glory. "Being in the form of God," St. Paul tells us, He "emptied Himself, taking the form of a servant, being made in the likeness of men; and being found in fashion as a man, He humbled Himself, becoming obedient even unto . . . the death of the cross."[1] To reveal Himself to us and make possible the fulfilment of our eternal destiny, God had to wrap His glory and greatness in such swaddling bands of weakness. This He alone could do, and only thus could He come to man and man attain to Him. So He wore our mortal flesh, was wrapped in swaddling clothes, and was laid in a manger.

> Partaker of the human name,
> He knows the frailty of our frame.[2]

Now the important thing from our point of view is not only that our Lord was made flesh, but that He accepted willingly all the limitations which mortality implied. Read the account of His life and one cannot but be impressed by the fact that Jesus stubbornly refused to live outside the narrow limits of human weakness. After His baptism in the wilderness, again after Peter's great confession, in the Garden of Gethsemane, and even on the Cross itself, the temptation to claim immunity from human limitations was ever present to Him, yet each time He rejected it. Jesus accepted His manhood even to the point of suffering and humiliation and death.

Is there not a salutary lesson for all in this fact? To be a man is not to be a superman, though some would like to think so. Our very humanity means that we

---

[1] Philippians 2:6-8. (R.V.)
[2] Scottish Paraphrases 58.

too are wrapped in swaddling bands of weakness, and if the Christ of God had to endure cold and hunger, exhaustion and weariness, if He wept bitter tears and sweated blood and endured the agony and anguish of the Cross, not one of us has any right to be surprised when life proves harder than we anticipated and the burden almost more than we can bear. We are men, not gods. We are frail creatures,

> Frail as summer's flower we flourish;
> Blows the wind and it is gone;[1]

And this frailty we must accept, not rebel against it as some do, to their own undoing. God asks nothing more of us than this, though ofttimes we ask much more of ourselves.

It is told of James the Fifth of Scotland that on occasion he would lay aside the royal robe of king and put on the simple clothes of the peasant. In such a disguise, he would move freely about the land, making friends with ordinary folk, entering into their difficulties, appreciating their handicaps, sympathizing with them in their sorrow. And when as king he sat again upon the throne, he was better able to rule over them with fatherly compassion and mercy. It was this and more than this which the King of Kings did on our behalf. He took upon Himself the form of a man, and limited Himself to the narrow bounds of mortal frailty.

Turn now to another group of garments which our Lord wore, *the clothes of His own choosing*, what the evangelists describe as "His own clothes". As far as we can gather, these clothes had nothing unusual or

[1] Henry Francis Lyte, "Praise, My Soul, the King of Heaven".

outré about them, for Jesus chose to dress Himself in the ordinary familiar peasant's garb of the time. He sought no distinction which clothes might give Him, but was content to be numbered among the great multitude of the common people.

That surely was typical of His whole life and ministry. He busied Himself for nigh on thirty years at the common trade of a carpenter. His home was an ordinary workman's dwelling. His friends were chosen from the everyday run of people. His greatest works were performed not before the eyes of the high, the mighty, the privileged, but invariably for the strengthening and encouragement and comfort of the great masses of ordinary folk, the common people who might well have come out of any great city or countryside the world over.

Nothing more clearly illustrates this whole emphasis of His ministry than the manner and method of His own teaching. When He who was God's Son clothed His message in the language of mortal speech, He chose the common tongue of men, the simplest forms of speech, the most familiar images and similes. That is why anyone can understand the Gospels, though it takes much patient study to grasp the significance of Paul's letters or of the Old Testament prophets. Christ clothes His message in the language of everyman, the language familiar to the child and the countryman, the simplicity of which is divine.

We must not, however, underestimate this simplicity. Jesus of Nazareth had far fewer worldly possessions than any one of us, and everything that was His was transformed and transfigured by His very use of it. By the touch of His hand, he could cleanse disease and restore life; but the touch of His garments was just as effective. His clothes as well as his face shone with heavenly light on the Mount of Transfiguration, while though the garment of His speech was simple, the glory with which He invested it shall never pass away so long as man walks the earth.

Human life may be a frail and weak thing, a reed shaken in the wind, yet with Christ's example before us it need never be a broken or worthless reed. We mortals may have to walk a very narrow path, but it is possible to do so with real nobility and dignity and grace. For ordinary common clothes, whether they be the clothes which cover our bodies or invest our thoughts or display our actions, can be made to reveal an abiding value, a lasting and indeed an everlasting greatness.

Here, indeed, is one of those things which Christ is always doing for those who acknowledge His lordship in life. He gives to common things an uncommon value. When Christian arrived at the Cross, three shining ones met him. The first brought forgiveness and the third gave him a map for the road. But the second stripped him of his rags and clothed him in a change of raiment[1] so that eventually when Christian and Faithful arrived at the city of Vanity Fair, their clothes gave them a distinction and marked them off from the citizens of that place. "The pilgrims," says Bunyan, "were clothed with such kind of raiment as was diverse from the raiment of any that traded in that fair."[2]

How often the coming of Christ into a human life has meant just this, a change of raiment! Go into any slum area where the evangel is being preached, and

[1] John Bunyan, *The Pilgrim's Progress.*
[2] Ibid.

you will find examples of this transforming grace on
every hand. Let the love of Christ constrain a dweller
in slumdom, and within a few weeks a new suit of
clothes, a new dress displaces the old rags. Put on
Jesus Christ, and we very soon discover that we must
clothe this body which is His temple with new garments; we must clothe thought in new language; we
must clothe our acts in new restraints and disciplines.

Clothes are significant, especially those clothes
which we choose for ourselves. For they do reflect the
soul and are transformed by the spirit dwelling within.
"Beware," says Thoreau, "of all enterprises that re-
quire new clothes, and not rather a new wearer of
clothes."[1] No one can give Jesus Christ the hospitality
of his heart and not find that the glory of the Lord is
reflected even in the clothes he wears.

> So for thy spirit did devise
> Its Maker seemly garniture . . .
> For outward robes in their ostents
> Should show the soul's habiliments.[2]

There remains a third group of clothes which our
Lord had to wear, *those clothes of others' choosing,* the
garments which others compelled Him to put on.

Two instances of this are given by the evangelists
and both occurred at the very end of His life. After
Pilate had unwillingly passed sentence of death upon
Him, Jesus was removed by the soldiers to the barrack
room of the Roman Governor's palace, and while they
waited there for the carpenters to finish their work
upon the cross, those rough legionaries carried through

[1] Henry David Thoreau, *Walden.*

[2] Francis Thompson, *Gilded Gold.* Burns, Oates & Washbourne Ltd. Courtesy Sir Francis Meynell.

the brutal sport of mocking the Prisoner. They clothed
Him in a gorgeous robe of purple and scarlet. They
plaited a crown of thorns and placed it on His head.
They put a palm branch in His hand, and they mocked
Him. "He was thus mocked," says Matthew Henry,
"not in His own clothes but in another's to signify that
He suffered not for His own sin." Then, when the play
was ended and the cross was ready, they led Him forth
to die clad "in His own clothes". That same night
Joseph of Arimathea clothed our Lord in other clothes
not of His own choosing. He wrapped that broken
body in a clean linen cloth and laid it to rest in his
own tomb.

What those Roman soldiers did in sport and mockery has been done again and again across the centuries
sometimes in jest but more often in earnest. Mankind
has so often refused to accept Christ in His own clothes,
in the garments of His own choosing. They have
insisted upon dressing Him up, upon adorning Him in
gorgeous liveries and startling vestures. Behind much
of this has lain the desire to honour Christ, to exalt
Him and glorify Him. All the pageantry and pomp of
so much worship is simply an attempt to exalt Him
whose name is Wonderful and do honour to Him who
is "very God of very God".

Yet what has so often happened has been the very
reverse of what was intended. Instead of revealing
the Lord, we have so often hidden Him. The clothes
have become more important than the wearer. The
creeds have supplanted the Christ, and with our systems of theology and our splendours of ritual we have
so often raised up an impenetrable barrier around the
Person of the Living Lord. Indeed, living religion has
only survived, because from time to time there have

been men and women courageous enough to strip from
Him those garments with which others have sought to
adorn Him. For these pioneers have always known
that religion is much more than ritual, much more than
correct notions and consistent creeds. Religion if it is
to be a living thing must be personal contact with a
personal Lord and Master.

It is not by adorning Jesus that we glorify Him,
but by accepting Him as He is and was and ever shall
be. Those clothes with which we would honour Him
are forever wearing thin and must be discarded. But
the clothes which He has chosen for Himself never pass
away. "In our era," wrote Thomas Carlyle in *Sartor
Resartus,* "those same Church-clothes have gone sor-
rowfully out-at-elbows; nay, far worse, many of them
have become mere hollow shapes, under which no
living figure or Spirit any longer dwells." Yet religion
is not dead, for, as he adds, "in unnoticed nooks (she)
is weaving for herself new vestures, wherewith to re-
appear, and bless us, or our sons and grandsons."[1]

Let no one, then, be repelled by the robe in which
Christ is presented to him. Jesus is greater than any
dress of language or ritual in which we may invest
Him. He is far bigger than all our creeds and confessions, far more wonderful and majestic and gracious
and divine than the most gorgeous pageantry of the
greatest cathedral. Let none of us rest content until
we have come to discover Him for ourselves, and not
simply the clothes in which men adorn Him: for only
when we have converse with His spirit, not simply
contact with His garments, can we find peace.

And this wonder of wonders is possible for all, for
at the very end of His life He put off His clothes, the

[1] Thomas Carlyle, *Sartor Resartus,* Bk. 3: ch. 2.

clothes of His own choosing and the clothes of God's choosing, so that His spirit is no more trammelled by the temporal and the mortal, and we who love Him and would serve Him can abide in Him and He in us. In Paul's pregnant phrase, we can "put on Christ Jesus".[1] We can make our mortal bodies His vesture in time, and live the glorious, victorious life of the Son of God because Christ lives in us.

> Mine is the sin, but Thine the righteousness;
> Mine is the guilt, but Thine the cleansing blood;
> Here is my robe, my refuge, and my peace—
> Thy blood, Thy righteousness, O Lord my God.[2]

[1] Romans 13:14; Galatians 3:27.
[2] Horatius Bonar, "Here O my Lord, I see Thee face to face".

IV

HIS HANDS

Behold my hands!

Sт. Luke 24:39. (Cf. St. John 20:27)

MANKIND has always found a peculiar fascination in the study of hands. The practice of palmistry, for instance, is one of the most ancient systems by which the superstitious hope to surprise the secrets of the future hidden in human hands. Three thousand years before Christ, the Chinese were endeavouring to foretell events by reading hands, and though today we know that this whole practice is based upon nothing but a fantastic imagination, nevertheless, like most superstitions, it covers a modicum of truth. Much can be learned about a person by a study of his hands.

Hands with long, tapered fingers immediately suggest the musician or the surgeon. Hard, horny hands belong to the labourer and the artisan. There are the folded hands of resignation, the chubby small hands of infants, the clenched hands of the rebel, the thin, wasted hands of the invalid. Study a man's hands and there is much you can learn about the man himself.

Furthermore, of all the instruments with which God has equipped us, our hands are by far the most creative and the most powerful. "The work of our hands" is indeed a phrase charged with almost endless meaning. Behind all the good that has been achieved in this world are human hands. They too have been the instruments to create and let loose the most appalling forces of evil and of destruction on the earth.

32

Hands save life and destroy it. They create beauty and goodness, but they also ravage and shatter them.

Look, then, at the hands of Jesus, the hands of the greatest of the sons of men; for we may be sure that the good He did with them, the use He made of them, the power that impelled them while He was here among men, remains the same forever. "The Lord's hand is not shortened that it cannot save",[1] and when after His resurrection, His own men doubted the very evidence of their own eyes, He shewed them His hands. "Reach hither thy finger, and behold my hands",[2] He pleaded with Thomas, for only our Lord has hands like these. They identify Him to His friends and followers.

To begin with, the hands of Christ were first and last the hands of a workman, a labourer, a toiler, and for the better part of thirty years He used them day and daily at Joseph's bench in the carpenter's shop in Nazareth. They knew the bite of frost and the browning of the sun. They were bruised and hurt and broken by the tree and the wood and the grain. The Cross was not the first occasion on which they were pierced, as Millais reminds us in his famous picture of "Christ in the Carpenter's Shop". Many a nail caught in His hand and tore it, and many a time Mary was on her knees at His side binding up the wound.

But the toiler's hands grew strong and steady and sure. Through long practice they gained great skill. They have become, indeed, hands that you and I can safely trust in any emergency, hands that can be as gentle as a child's and yet as firm and strong as a vice.

[1] Isaiah 59:1.
[2] St. John 20:27.

How glad Simon Peter must have been of those two tried hands that night when walking the waters first his faith and then his foothold failed, and the strong hands of Christ took hold upon him and dragged him back from the devouring deep. They will not fail us, those strong hands of Christ. They have power to hold us even when we have no power to hold them. They drag us back from many a terrible pit and save us from many a nameless disaster.

Little wonder, then, that we sing with such exultant joy that great hymn of George Matheson's, "O Love that wilt not let me go!" Not even the devil himself can pry open those strong fingers when they lay hold upon us, for when Christ Jesus takes hold of a man or of a woman, He never lets them go. Indeed, the whole secret of Christian victory might be summed up as being the complete surrender of ourselves to the hand and hold of Christ. Long ago the Psalmist found peace in the knowledge that God's hand was upon him. "If I take the wings of the morning," he wrote, "and dwell in the uttermost parts of the sea; even there shall thy hand lead me, and thy right hand shall hold me!"[1] It was the same counsel which Loyola gave to his army of followers. "Be like a stick in a man's hand," he told them. And another great disciple, Richard Baxter, confessed on his death bed, when his friends praised the great achievements of his life: "I was but a pen in His hand, and what praise is due to a pen?" And then he added, "All His saints are in His hands."[2]

To be in the hands of Christ, there is the secret of security and strength, of peace and victory, of rest and achievement. "Behold my hands!" He says to

[1] Psalm 139:9-10.

[2] Rita Snowden, *If I Open My Door*. The Epworth Press.

us. They are strong hands, mighty to save and mighty
to keep. They are the only hands that you can trust
through time and through eternity,—hands that will
never let you go!

But the Master's hands were not only strong in
their grasp; they were also potent in their power, for
they were the healing, helping hands of the Good
Physician, the hands of the Lord of Life, the mighty
Conqueror of disease and death.

The Gospels are packed full with stories of how
the sick were brought to Jesus and He healed them.
The blind came and He anointed their eyes so that
sight was restored. Lepers grovelled at His feet and
His touch cleansed them. The dead rose again to new
life when His hands were laid upon them. The scourge
of leprosy, the night of blindness, the chains of disease,
the frozen stillness of death all melted and vanished
away before the wonder of His touch. In all the long
history of mankind, never have there been hands so
potent to heal, so mighty to save as these hands of
Jesus. They are the cleansing, curing, restoring hands
of the world's Saviour that leave beauty in place of
loathsome ugliness and bring the bloom of life and
health where before only the pallor of death has
reigned.

The Jesus Who holds, also saves. The Lord Who
touches, transforms and transfigures whatever He
touches. A modern school has attempted to gloss over
and spiritualize the miracles of Jesus. Yet the truth is
that hardly any facts about His life are so well attested.
He was the great Miracle Worker to His contemporaries, and for countless thousands throughout the ages
He remains the Great Healer, the potent Physician for

body and mind and spirit. Indeed, as the late Professor D. S. Cairns has well argued, if only we could recover that first century quality of faith in the Lord, we too could remove mountains; we too could turn many a dark and dread handicap of this mortal life into a glorious triumph.

But we must not speak as if such faith does not exist. It does; and across the world vast multitudes of men and women are facing life with courage and grace and confidence because they have believed and have through faith known the helping healing touch of the Lord upon them. Because His "touch has still its ancient power" the unclean has been rendered sterile in many a life; the crippling burden has been wonderfully lightened; and the awful cross that once had power to crucify us has flowered into a new and infinitely more radiant life. These things are true, witnessed to by a multitude of men and women who have become "more than conquerors through Him that loved them".[1]

> For lo! Thy touch brought life and health
> Gave speech, and strength and sight;
> And youth renewed and frenzy calmed
> Owned Thee the Lord of Light.[2]

Let Him touch you, then! Resign yourself to those strong hands, you who are morally and mentally and spiritually halt and lame and blind, hopelessly crippled in this race of life and bowed down beneath intolerable burdens. Let Christ touch you. Let Him put the strong hand of His love upon you and you shall live!

[1] Romans 8:37.

[2] Edward Hayes Plumptre: "Thine arm, O Lord, in days of old".

Look again at those hands of Jesus, for we have not yet considered the most distinctive thing about them. "Behold my hands!" He says to His followers, and they see there the print of the nails. "Take my hand!" He invites, and you know at once whose hand it is that you hold. There is hardly anything of which we are more sensitive than the feel of a person's hands, and there can be no mistaking Christ's hands. We shall always know them by the feel of the nail prints in them.

When Thomas Cranmer burned at the stake, he thrust first into the fire that hand which had subscribed to the false doctrine of papal supremacy. "This hand hath offended," he cried, "this unworthy hand!" But those pierced hands were never unworthy hands, but clean and pure. There was a day in Edinburgh many years ago when a pair of clean pure hands were fixed on the spikes at the Netherbow, the hands of Richard Cameron, the Covenanter. On the morning of his death, he had asked for water to wash his hands. "It is their last washing," he remarked, "I have need to make them clean, for there are many to see them."[1] And they were clean hands which hung on Calvary's Cross, hands that had brought blessing to little children, health to the diseased, life to the dead, but above all cleansing and forgiveness to the sinner. No other hands could do this for us, and none were ever so clean.

It was by His hands that our Lord hung to the Cross. He might have refused. He might have come down and saved Himself, but He would not spare His own life and claimed instead a criminal's death that He might open heaven's gate and let us in! Dr. Hubert

[1] John MacBeath, *Taken Unawares*. Pickering & Inglis.

Simpson has told of a little girl who, returning from school one day, caused consternation in her home by saying that she had been punished by her teacher for the first time in her life. Pressed to give the reason for the punishment, she confessed to a particularly grave fault. "But you never did a thing like that!" her mother protested. "No, of course I didn't," came the answer, "but no one would own up, and something had to be done about it, so I held up my hand." That is what happened on Calvary. Something had to be done about our human sin and sinfulness and our Lord held up His hands for our sakes.

"Behold my hands!" cries Jesus, and well He knows that we can never look upon them without knowing that they are the hands of One Who has loved us with an everlasting love. Nor can we ever feel them tug at our coat sleeve or knock at our heart's door and not realize the immortal victory that is theirs. The pierced hands of Love are the most potent hands in this universe. On one occasion, following unspeakable sufferings in a filthy prison, Adoniram Judson appeared before the King of Burma and asked permission to go to a certain city to preach. "I am willing for a dozen preachers to go, but not you," was the answer. "Not with those hands! My people are not such fools as to take notice of your preaching, but they will take notice of those scarred hands."[1] And the whole world must take notice of the pierced hands of Christ, the hands that cleansed, the hands that were held high for us on Calvary, the hands that alone can knock at the human heart and persuade us to open the innermost places of

[1] Rita Snowden, *If I Open My Door*. The Epworth Press.

life to His reign and rule. For, in the words of Studdert
Kennedy,

> The Christ who was born on Christmas Day
> Laid on the world his two small hands,
> Lifting it worlds and worlds away
> Up to the level of Love's demands.[1]

Thus we come to the last thought of all suggested
by the hands of Jesus. Those hands that were tested
in toiling, that were mighty to heal, that were lifted
up to be pierced for our sakes, those hands remain
forevermore uplifted in blessing upon the children of
men. St. Luke tells us that the last vision the disciples
had of their Master was a vision of His hands lifted
high in blessing. "And He led them out as far as to
Bethany, and He lifted up His hands and blessed them.
And while He blessed them, He was parted from them
and carried up into heaven."[2] The eternal Christ is
the Christ of blessing Whose hands are raised over us
in benediction.

Is it possible that any of us have remained unaware
of that blessing? Is it possible that we have mistaken
it for something other than it is? Old Anna was wiser
than many of us as she sat in her chimney corner
comforting Eliza. " 'Listen dear,' Anna said, 'God's
arm is not shortened. . . . God takes a han' wherever
He can find it, and jist diz what He likes wi' it. Sometimes He takes a bishop's and lays it on a child's head
in benediction, then He takes the han' of a dochter t'
relieve pain, th' han' of a mother t' guide her chile, an'

[1] Op. cit.
[2] St. Luke 24:50.

sometimes He takes th' han' of an aul' craither like me t' give a bit comfort to a neighbour. But they're all han's touch't by His Spirit, an' His Spirit is everywhere lukin' for han's to use.' "[1]

"All hands touched by His Spirit." Then are yours? Are mine? Have we put our hands into the hand of Christ?

> Hold Thou my hands!
> In grief and joy, in hope and fear,
> Lord, let me feel that Thou art near:
> Hold Thou my hands!
>
> And when at length,
> With darkened eyes and fingers cold,
> I seek some last loved hand to hold,
> Hold Thou my hands![2]

[1] Alexander Irvine, *My Lady of the Chimney Corner*. William Collins Sons & Co., Ltd.

[2] William Canton, "Hold Thou my hands!"

V

HIS MOUTH

Never man spake like this man.

St. John 7:46.

Out of his mouth went a sharp two-edged sword.

Revelation 1:16.

He was oppressed and he was afflicted, yet he opened
not his mouth.

Isaiah 53:7.

ONE OF the cleverest if more cynical definitions of the
word "mouth" is that attributed to Ambrose Bierce,
the colorful American satirist and poet of half-a-century
ago. In his *Devil's Dictionary* he describes mouth as
"in man, the gateway to the soul; in woman, the outlet
of the heart".[1] By the change of one word, it seems
to me that we get nearer the truth, for there is a real
sense in which the mouth is "the gateway *of* the soul,
and the outlet of the heart". "Speech," declared one
of the ancients, "is the mirror of the soul: as the man,
so is his speech."[2]

In passing, however, we must not ignore the bio-
logical function which the mouth fulfils. By means of
it the physical body is nourished, and though there are
few references to our Lord's use of His mouth in this
way, we do know that He too required to be fed and
nourished like every ordinary mortal. Indeed, the
insistent demands of His body to be fed and nourished
were ever present. The first of His temptations was to

[1] Ambrose Bierce, *Devil's Dictionary*. Profile Press.
[2] Publilius Syrus, *Sententiae No. 1073*.

41

turn stones into bread, for Jesus knew the gnawing pains of hunger, and was familiar with those evils which run at the heels of the wolf of starvation. To the end of life He accepted this physical frame with its clamorous needs, nor did they leave Him until the last breath had fled from His body. It was from the cross that there came the great cry of the flesh, "I thirst."[1] He who had begun His ministry experiencing the pangs of hunger ended it in the anguish of thirst.

It is not primarily with the physical use to which He put His mouth that we are concerned here, but rather with the spiritual purposes which it served. Out of His mouth, Jesus gave us His message, and because of the words which flowed from His lips, we have come to know Him as the Incarnate Word of God to the human race. No organ of His body was of greater importance than this organ which He made the gateway of His soul and the outlet of His heart.

First among all uses to which our Lord put His mouth was, of course, that of preaching. By means of it He proclaimed God's truth and propagated the good news among men.

Jesus never wrote a book. There was only one occasion on which we know that He wrote and then it was upon the unsubstantial unrecording dust. Though He had the greatest of all messages to give, yet He refused to take the ordinary precautions that would have preserved it, and instead was content to commit it in words to the ears of His hearers. "Jesus came preaching",[2] not writing. It is one of the amazing things in history. "It pleased God," says St. Paul, "by

[1] St. John 19:28.
[2] St. Mark 1:14.

the foolishness of preaching to save them that believe."[1]

But what preaching it was! The multitudes hung upon His words. "The common people heard Him gladly." Once when soldiers came to arrest Him, they returned without their prisoner to give the incredible reason, so incredible that it must be true, that they could not arrest Him because "never man spake like this man."[2] Surely we have here the explanation why, though He wrote no book, so many of His words have been preserved for us. Once men heard them from His lips, there could be no forgetting them. They remained indelibly etched upon the table of men's minds. They were written upon something more durable than paper, for they were written into the very lives of His hearers.

One of the penalties of being born in a Christian home and being reared in a Christian land is that these "wonderful words of Jesus" are so often allowed to grow tarnished as they are bandied about from tongue to tongue. Our overfamiliarity with them has stripped them of their sterling freshness and revolutionary import. Yet not all our cheap handling of them can destroy their power nor rob them of their immortal beauty and grace. After two thousand years and against the background of all human history, it still remains true that "never man spake like this man", and with His fellow-citizens in Nazareth, we too bear witness and wonder "at the gracious words which proceeded out of His mouth."[3]

It is not only, however, as a wonderful teacher and master in the use of words that we remember Him, but

[1] I Corinthians 1:21.
[2] St. John 7:46.
[3] St. Luke 4:22.

because no human words ever carried a richer or a more precious content. When He spoke, men listened not just because He had power to hold their rapt attention, but because in all that He said there was a note of finality never heard before. His hearers "were astonished at His doctrine: for He taught them as one that had authority, and not as the scribes."[1] To listen to Jesus was to know that you were in the presence of one who knew of what He spoke. Here was no petty debater placing before His audience the "pros" and "cons" of a case. Here was no mere reporter passing on second-hand information. Here was one who spoke as God speaks, with an absolute authority, with an unquestioning assurance, with a divine finality. No wonder the hierarchy of the Jewish Church hated him! If He was not God, then He deserved their hatred. For only God dare speak as Christ did; only God can speak as Christ did.

We cannot here consider the message which His words carried, but we must recall how potent it was. By the words of His lips, Jesus banished disease, silenced the ravings of the insane, summoned the dead back from their graves. Through words, He forgave the sinner, inspired courage in the fearful, comforted the broken-hearted, and kindled undying faith in the hearts of followers and friends. With words, He made for Himself claims unparalleled in the records of man's spirit. Caiaphas and Annas, with the rest of the Sanhedrin, could never have condemned Him had He not condemned Himself. "Art thou the Son of God?" they asked in final desperation. "Certainly, I am," came the ringing reply. "What more evidence do we need?" they asked, "We have heard it from His own

[1] St. Mark 1:22.

lips."[1] Out of His own mouth, He was judged, and from His own lips came those stupendous claims which have shaken the world.

"Never man spake like this man." It is still true. Then do we know His words, and like the Psalmist make them "a lamp unto our feet and a light unto our path"?[2] "I hope in thy word," said this Old Testament saint. "The entrance of thy words giveth light; it giveth understanding unto the simple . . . Order my steps in thy word."[3] The words of Jesus are the words of life, but only when they have taken root within the human heart, only when they have been woven into the very texture of our thought and word and deed. "Whosoever heareth these sayings of mine and doeth them," said Jesus, "I will liken him unto a wise man, which built his house upon a rock . . . and it fell not."[4] Have we not all need to pray that we be doers of the word as well as hearers of it?

Another use to which our Lord put the words of His mouth claims notice. He made them the instrument of judgment. In the Revelation of St. John we have a vision of the eternal Christ, and "out of his mouth went a sharp two-edged sword."[5] That was true of His earthly ministry, as it remains true of His everlasting destiny. Out of his mouth there comes the sword of judgment.

Throughout His life, Jesus was constantly surrounded by enemies. Lawyers, professors from Jewish

[1] St. Luke 22:70-71 (Moffatt).
[2] Psalm 119:105.
[3] Psalm 119:114, 130, 133.
[4] St. Matthew 7:24-25.
[5] Revelation 1:16.

colleges, emissaries of the Sanhedrin as well as ordinary doubting Thomases were constantly setting snares in order to trap Him. Casually a man would come to Him with a Roman coin bearing Caesar's head upon it. Is he to pay tribute to a heathen Emperor? It sounds harmless enough. Yet if Jesus should answer "Yes", then He would be no friend of the oppressed Jews. On the other hand, if He answered negatively, He could be accused of fomenting rebellion. You remember the answer which He did give, "Render unto Caesar the things which are Caesar's; and unto God the things that are God's."[1]

The words of His mouth reveal His mastery in debate, His brilliance in the art of controversy. Yet nowhere do we find Him fighting mere wordy battles for the sake of vanquishing an opponent. Always He used controversy to bring forth the deeper truths of His message as well as to uncover the specious plans of His enemies. Many of His greatest sayings, many of His most memorable parables owe their origin to some such occasion. Even in the heat of debate, He refused to lose sight of His mission, and by the gift that was in Him turned every opportunity to the service of His Gospel.

Part of the task to which Christ calls His followers is that of arming themselves for those battles which His enemies are constantly forcing upon us. Yet too often we have been slow to learn this lesson and have gone forth like lambs among wolves. Christian apologetics, that branch of theology whose business it is to answer the critics, has become very much the province of a few specialist theologians instead of the parade ground for every active soldier. Today especially is

[1] St. Matthew 22:21.

there need for the disciples of Christ to equip themselves for this battle. It is our privilege and duty to give back the Christian answer when the sciences or the pseudo-sciences, the biologist or the psychologist, would seek to sweep away Christianity with a syllogism. Then there is the increasing pressure of the attack which comes from the political theories of the age, from the new religions of Communism and Nationalism and Racialism. Have we the Christian answer? There is one, have no doubt on that point. Yet too few possess it for the strengthening of their own faith.

The Church of Jesus Christ has grown strongest in the hours of her fiercest controversies. Here is the whetstone on which the sword of the spirit can be sharpened, and ofttimes God in His wisdom allows us to be sore set upon by enemies in order that we may find again how secure is our foothold and how unshakeable are the foundations of faith in the Rock of Ages.

There is of course another sense in which Christ's words judge us. They judge us as the ideal judges the real, as truth judges falsehood, as goodness judges evil. Every word that He uttered becomes a judgment upon each of us, for like all the greatest achievements of the human spirit, it is not Jesus who is on trial as we hear His words, but we who hear, we who listen. In his judgment of the nations, the prophet Amos startled and staggered the people of his own land by declaring that their judgment would be all the more searching, because of their privilege as the people of God. And that remains true. To have received this glorious Gospel, to hold in our hands an open Bible, to have free access to the words of Christ: all that means a correspondingly heavy responsibility and a more terrible judgment, if we should neglect so great salvation. "The words that I speak unto you," declared Jesus, "they are spirit and they are life."[1] Are we who have heard them living in the spirit? Have we found and made our own the life that is in them? If not, then how indeed can we escape God's righteous judgment?

Turn now to a small group of incidents recorded by the evangelists in which our Lord, contrary to His practice, refused to open His mouth, occasions when He stood silent in the presence of others.

That happened when He was brought before Herod. It is the silence of Christ in the presence of a carnal worldling, the silence of God before a man incapable of reverence and utterly devoid of the "fear of the Lord". To such a person Jesus has nothing to say. What use is there trying to describe the beauty of a sunset to a blind man who refuses to believe that the sun exists? Nor is there any purpose in speaking to a soul so imprisoned in the gross darkness of its own sin that it cannot and will not believe in the possibility of any other form of life. Herod was like that. The only realities to him were sensual gratification and brutal tyranny, and before such a man Jesus of Nazareth stands silent. God forbid that any of us should ever find ourselves cast into such outer darkness where even the Saviour of the world cannot reach us nor help us!

Then we have the silence of Jesus as He stood before Pilate. His silence there amazed the Roman Procurator. Nothing like this had ever happened in his long experience. "Hearest thou not how many

[1] St. John 6:63.

things they witness against thee?"[1] Pilate asked in wonderment. The Prisoner's silence baffled and confused him, for it was the silence, not of condemnation, but of submission. In that hour our Lord knew that now He must die and the forces of evil would have their way with Him. No longer were mere words of any avail. Words could not stem the awful tide of evil's fury. Only deeds could do that; only a cross could do that. So He held His peace, He kept His silence. "As a sheep before her shearers is dumb, so he openeth not his mouth."[2]

Here is the royal, kingly silence of the Lamb of God, who taketh away the sin of the world, the silence of the great High Priest as He enters the Holy of Holies to make a sacrifice for the sins of mankind. It is the awful silence of the Love of God that fell across the universe like the pall of death on that Good Friday night only to be broken by the glory of Easter Morning when the cry went up, "He is Risen!"[3] "If thou, Lord, shouldest mark iniquities, O Lord, who shall stand?"[4] cries the Psalmist. Had the Lord spoken in that hour of His judgment what judgment could He have uttered but to condemn us for ever? So He kept silence that our race might be spared.

Then there is the other recorded instance of Christ's silence, His silence before the woman taken in sin and brought before Him for judgment. Jesus refused to judge her. Instead He wrote upon the sand, wrote until the last of her accusers had slunk away in shame

[1] St. Matthew 27:13.
[2] Isaiah 53:7.
[3] St. Matthew 28:6.
[4] Psalm 130:3.

and only she was left. Then He spoke and the words on His lips were mercy and love and life. "Neither do I condemn thee. Go and sin no more."[1]

Someday you and I must appear before the judgment seat of Christ, and if He shall speak, who will stand? But I know my Saviour well. I know that where sin abounds grace doth much more abound. I know that love will seal His lips, and that we who have deserved death shall find life. For when our sins parade before Him in their hideous liveries and accuse us, then He who died for us will hold His peace. There will be silence in heaven. Even the angels will cease their singing and hold their breath to hear His word. And that word will be life and immortality for you and me. For the silence will at last be broken, and out of His lips shall come salvation. "My brother, my sister," we shall hear Him say, "neither do I condemn thee. Go, go into all eternity, and sin no more."

[1] St. John 8:11.

VI

HIS EYES

Jesus looked round about.

St. Mark 10:23.

And the Lord turned and looked (in) upon Peter.

St. Luke 22:61.

Jesus lifted up his eyes and said, Father.

St. John 11:41.

Sight is one of the greatest of God's gifts, and the organs of sight, the eyes, among the most beautiful. The artist delights to paint them, the novelist to dwell upon them, the poet to praise them, the lover to gaze into them. Eyes are in a real sense windows to the soul, jewelled windows by which the spirit looks out upon the world and the world looks in upon the soul. In an essay on "Physiognomy" in his volume *Stray Leaves of Literature,* John Saunders declares that "whatever of goodness emanates from the soul gathers its soft halo in the eyes: and if the heart be a lurking-place of crime, the eyes are sure to betray the secret. A beautiful eye makes silence eloquent, a kind eye makes contradiction assent, an enraged eye makes beauty a deformity."[1]

Our Lord was fully aware of the significance of this tiny organ and of the influence which it exerts. "The light of the body is the eye", He told His disciples; "if therefore thine eye be single, thy whole body shall be full of light. But if thine eye be evil, thy whole

---

[1] John Saunders, *Stray Leaves of Literature.*

body shall be full of darkness. If therefore the light that is in thee be darkness, how great is that darkness."[1] That is to say, the use we make of our eyes is the determining factor as to whether or not we are to possess the true light of life. Earlier in the Sermon on the Mount, He had spoken of the evil of the lustful eye, and gave the stern warning, "If thy right eye offend thee, pluck it out and cast it from thee: for it is profitable for thee that one of thy members should perish, and not that thy whole body should be cast into hell."[2]

He who had so deep and far-reaching a knowledge of the part which the eye plays in the life of the soul was Himself a master in its use, and many are the references in Scripture as to how He employed it. There is much to learn, then, from studying the eyes of our Lord and the uses to which He put them.

Jesus used His eyes, and no one could ever accuse Him of "seeing but not perceiving". His eyes were open to see farther and look deeper than any other pair of eyes ever possessed by mortal man. Writing of Charles Dickens, Walter Bagehot tells of the great novelist's amazing powers of vision. Dickens, he declares, "could go down a crowded street and tell you all that was in it, what each shop was, what the grocer's name was, how many scraps of orange peel there were on the pavement. His works give you exactly the same idea. The amount of detail which there is in them is something amazing and to an ordinary writer something incredible."[3]

[1] St. Matthew 6:22-23.
[2] St. Matthew 5:29.
[3] *The Speaker's Bible*, St. Luke Vol. II, James Hastings, ed.

In a similar way, our Lord had this same power of vision. He too saw everything, the lilies in the field, the fowls of the air, the sparrows in the market-place, the changing splendours and warnings of the sky. There was nothing that happened in home or city or countryside which escaped those all-seeing eyes. He remembered the way bread was baked and clothes patched; how the farmer sowed and weeded and reaped; how new wine was stored and what wages were paid by the husbandman. Like a bright searchlight those eyes discovered everything, remembered everything.

Knowing the value which He placed upon the gift of sight, it is not surprising to find that Jesus spent much of His time opening the eyes of the blind. He who knew the blessing of eyes sought to bring that blessing to others. At His command blind Bartimaeus received his sight. The man born blind had his eyes anointed with clay by the Lord and after washing them in the pool of Siloam found his vision restored. When messengers came from John to Jesus, they were sent back with instructions to show John "those things which ye do hear and see," and first among them was the fact that "the blind receive their sight."[1] Wherever He went, the eyes of men, the eyes of the blind, the ignorant, the unbelieving, the eyes of strangers and friends, of beggars and disciples, were opened. Indeed, one of the last recorded facts concerning His earthly ministry is that He opened the eyes of two of His followers as He broke bread with them in the quiet of a home at Emmaus.

He whose eyes were ever open has been the great Opener of men's eyes. Because of all He did and was, we are able to look round about us with new perception

[1] St. Matthew 11:4-5.

and understanding. Jesus has helped us to look at all
of life from a new vantage-ground, so that mankind
has discovered new glories in nature, new wonders in
man, new horizons never before imagined. "Open your
eyes," cried Jacob Boehme, "and the whole world is
full of God." This, Christ has done for us. He has
shown us God's hand shaping the loveliness of every
flower and caring for the wild things of nature. He has
opened our eyes to see new and eternal values in little
children. He has made us look with compassion upon
the poor and helpless, upon the diseased and despised
among men. And He has made us lift up our eyes and
look across the earth to see that great and glorious
harvest of human life and love which waits to be
gathered in to the granaries of God.

No one can walk with Him and remain in the comfortable obscurity of blindness.

> He wakes desires you never may forget,
> > He shows you stars you never saw before,
> > He makes you share with him, for evermore,
> The burden of the world's divine regret.
> How wise you were to open not! and yet,
> > How poor if you should turn him from the door![1]

There can be no doubt that open eyes are not always
comfortable things to possess. It is much more comfortable to go through life seeing only what we want
to see. But Christ will have none of His followers do
that. Their eyes must be open to "share with him, for
evermore, the burden of the world's divine regret".

It was in His dealings, however, with other people
that our Lord's most startling use of His eyes is re-

[1] Sidney Royse Lysaght, "The Penalty of Love".

vealed. Men might come to Him singly or in crowds,
yet He was able to see what no other could see; for
Jesus had power not only to look upon the outward
condition but upon the inward character. When He
looked at a man, He also looked into the man, though
even the person concerned might not be aware of this
deep penetration of vision.

At the beginning of His public ministry, Nathaniel
was startled and surprised by this amazing insight
possessed by Christ. Again and again throughout His
ministry, the sick, the diseased, the insane were brought
to Him, and with one searching glance our Lord was
able to penetrate beyond the outward malady to the
inner spiritual rot which festered in the soul of the
suppliant. That day in the synagogue at Capernaum,
for example, onlookers were startled to hear Jesus say
to the man sick of palsy not "Take up thy bed and
walk," but "Son, thy sins are forgiven thee."[1] Yet the
invalid himself knew well that it was the cancer of
unforgiven sin which underlay his whole wretched
condition.

The eyes of Jesus looked into the very hearts and
souls of men. In one of His sermons, He spoke of there
being "nothing covered that shall not be revealed",
and nothing "hid that shall not be known".[2] That was
His own experience when He confronted His fellowmen.
Jesus saw the inward as well as the outward, and by a
glance could uncover the secret things of heart and
soul and spirit. Like a divine x-ray, His vision made
plain the innermost secrets of all hearts.

Little wonder that men quailed before those all-
seeing eyes! It is one of the great laws of the kingdom

[1] St. Mark 2:5.
[2] St. Luke 12:2.

of the spirit that those of lower spiritual attainment cannot look into the eyes of their masters. In *The Jungle Book*, Kipling reminds us how this holds true of the animal kingdom. Mowgli found it a hard lesson to learn when the wolf pack turned against him. " 'But why—but why should any wish to kill me?' he asked of his faithful friend, Bagheera, the black panther. 'Look at me,' said Bagheera; and Mowgli looked at him steadily between the eyes. The big panther turned his head away in half a minute. 'That is why,' he said. 'Not even I can look thee between the eyes, and I was born among men, and I love thee, Little Brother. The others they hate thee because their eyes cannot meet thine—because thou art wise—because thou hast pulled out thorns from their feet—because thou art a man.' "[1]

So it is when men stand before Christ. Sinners dare not look into His eyes. All they may do is cast themselves in shame at His feet, and the cry of Simon Peter is still the cry of mortal man when the eyes of Christ are upon him: "Depart from me; for I am a sinful man, O Lord."

Yet the eyes of Jesus dare to look upon us and therein lies our hope. One of the greatest problems of all human experience is that of being known and understood. Many of us do not even know ourselves. All we do know is that we are sick and in need of a physician. But where shall we find one wise enough to minister to our deepest needs? Where shall we find a physician for the soul as well as for the body, for the heart as well as for the mind? The answer of countless thousands out of every century, the answer which is

[1] Rudyard Kipling, *The Jungle Book*. Courtesy Mrs. George Bambridge, Messrs. A. P. Watt & Son, and The Macmillan Company of Canada Limited.

as true today as it was two thousand years ago in Galilee is that only at the feet of Christ, only before the eyes of Christ is there life and hope for us. We may not know ourselves, but He knows; for He sees into the innermost places of life. From Him nothing is hid, nothing is secret; and to those who resign themselves to His tender care and mercy, He brings life out of death, strength out of weakness, health out of sickness.

> All-Seeing Sight
> Cleaves through the husk of things,
> Right to the Roots and Springs,—
> Sees all things whole,
> And measures less the body than the soul.
> All-Righteous Right
> Will weigh men's motives,
> Not their deeds alone.
> End and Beginning unto Him are one;
> And *would* for *could* shall oft, perchance, atone.[1]

It is a terrible, a harrowing experience to stand before the eyes of Christ and have Him look into the very depths of your soul. But there is life and love and liberty in hearing Him say, "Son, Daughter, thy sins are forgiven thee."

The eyes of Jesus, however, not only looked out across the wide world and deep into the hearts of men; they also looked up to heaven and into the face of God. Many references in the Gospels speak of the uplifted eyes of the Master. He began the Sermon on the Mount by lifting up His eyes. Later He lifted up His eyes upon the multitudes when they followed Him into

[1] John Oxenham, *Bees in Amber*. Methuen & Co. Ltd.

the fastnesses of Galilee. But it is largely in reference to His prayer life that the evangelists speak of His eyes being lifted up. When the great stone was rolled away from over the grave of Lazarus, "Jesus lifted up His eyes and said, Father I thank Thee that Thou hast heard me."[1] Again in the Upper Room, when His teaching was ended, He "lifted up his eyes to heaven and said, Father, the hour is come."[2] It was characteristic of Christ's prayer life that His eyes were raised to heaven. He who had always looked with complete candour and honesty upon the world, looked with perfect confidence and unwavering faith to God His Father.

This, indeed, is the greatest thing Christ has done for His followers. He has opened their eyes to see horizons beyond all mortal reach. "It pleased God of His wonderful mercy," says Richard Baxter writing of his conversion, "to open my eyes with a clearer insight into the concerns and case of my own soul, and to touch my heart with a livelier feeling of things spiritual than ever I had found before."[3] Fall into step by the side of Christ, and He lifts the curtain from the temporal to unveil the eternal. No longer are the supreme realities the obvious, outward things of this world. Instead they are the hidden things of God. True, here we only "see through a glass darkly",[4] but we do see. We do "walk by faith, not by sight",[5] for "we look not at the things which are seen, but at the

---

[1] St. John 11:41.

[2] St. John 17:1.

[3] Richard Baxter, *Autobiography*.

[4] I Corinthians 13:12.

[5] II Corinthians 5:7.

things which are not seen: for the things which are
seen are temporal; but the things which are not seen
are eternal."[1]

The fact is that for Christ's disciples this world is
never more than an outward shell, a transient cage, a
mortal prison-house. The true and real world lies
beyond and above, and towards this we are ever
marching "looking unto Jesus the Author and Finisher
of our Faith".[2] For the day will come when "we shall
know even as also we are known"[3]; when "He shall
wipe away all tears from our eyes",[4] and we shall see
Him as He is.

> The Goal in sight! Look up and sing,
>   Set faces full against the light,
> Welcome with rapturous welcoming
>   The Goal in sight.

> Death hunts you, yea, but reft of sting;
>   Your bed is green, your shroud is white:
> Hail! Life and Death and all that bring
>   The Goal in sight.[5]

Yes, our eyes shall see Him, as His eyes see us. For
let us not forget that those eyes which scanned the
world and searched the souls of men and were uplifted
to the face of His Father are still looking out along the
ancient highways of life, watching for us to come home.
"I came to God's throne and found it wet with tears,"

[1] II Corinthians 4:18.
[2] Hebrews 12:2.
[3] I Corinthians 13:12.
[4] Revelation 21:4.
[5] Christina Rossetti, "The Goal in Sight".

wrote an old Covenanting woman. "And I said, 'O my Father, whose tears are these?' And He whispered gently, 'My child, I have waited long for thee. The tears are mine.'"

VII

HIS FACE

We all, with open face beholding as in a glass the glory of the Lord, are changed into the same image from glory to glory.

II CORINTHIANS 3:18.

The light of the knowledge of the glory of God in the face of Jesus Christ.

II CORINTHIANS 4:6.

IN ONE of the best known poems in the English language, Lord Tennyson has given expression to the awful finality of death in the cry of two familiar lines:

> But O for the touch of a vanish'd hand,
> And the sound of a voice that is still![1]

One wonders, however, if in such times our most passionate longing is not to see again, as Newman puts it,

> Those angel faces smile,
> Which I have loved long since and lost awhile.[2]

It is the human face, more than anything else, which mirrors the human soul, and among the most persistent and passionate desires of the heart is this desire to see the faces of those whom we love and honour and reverence.

For countless thousands, the sight of a human face has been the turning point in life, while many keep the face of some great hero or saint hanging before

[1] Lord Tennyson, "Break, Break, Break".
[2] John Henry Newman, "Lead, Kindly Light".

their eyes that they may draw inspiration and strength
from its noble lines. "All the greatest painting is of
the human face," declared Ruskin. "The human face
is my landscape," said Joshua Reynolds, and in truth
it is the only landscape in which our eyes can find
abiding rest. That brilliant American Platonist, Paul
Elmer More, discovered this when he found the world
of ideas and ideals pall upon him, until his soul was
encompassed in a dread and barren loneliness. "My
longing for some audible voice out of the infinite silence
rose to a pitch of torture," he confessed. "To be satisfied I must see face to face, I must, as it were, handle
and feel,—and how should this be?" It was only when
he came to Jesus Christ and to faith in the incarnation
of God in Him, that More came to find peace for his
own soul.

"I must see face to face." How many have uttered
that cry! Yet, when men seek to look upon the face
of Jesus Christ, an impenetrable veil appears to hide
Him from our eyes. This surely is one of the astounding facts of history. The one face which above all
others we want to see remains almost the only face we
cannot see. The artist is able to reconstruct for us the
features of Homer, of Virgil or of Shakespeare. All of
us are familiar with the ugliness of Socrates and the
"pale cast of thought" which distinguished Plato. The
face of Buddha is known the world over, while the
earth is littered with busts and portraits of kings and
princes. But the face of Jesus Christ remains hidden
behind the curtain of twenty centuries.

The traditional portrait of Christ has, of course, no
claim to authenticity. The late Professor R. G. Moul-
ton has told us how it is actually a reproduction of the

wonderful face of the Olympian Zeus with which Phidias startled the Athenian world of his day. Previously Zeus had always been portrayed in terrible majesty, brandishing a thunderbolt with which he would destroy the earth. Phidias, too, portrayed Zeus with a face of divine majesty, but for the first time it was the majesty of benevolence and fatherliness. Thus for five centuries before our Lord was laid in His cradle, that face which we now associate with Him looked out upon the world. In the Middle Ages, the statue of Zeus disappeared, but the face remained as the face of Jesus of Nazareth.

So with all would-be portraits of our Lord, none survive that are true. The fact is so striking as to challenge attention. Here, surely, we have no mere coincidence, but part of a divine ordering of things. It was not in the purposes of God that men should have any likeness of the Son of Man to turn to for inspiration and encouragement. We are required to walk by faith, not by sight. We are to discipline ourselves to look not upon the outward man but upon the inward spirit, and commune not with the flesh but with the soul.

The physical form of a face is, after all, no more than a mirror of the inward life, and the faces most dear to us are cherished and loved because we have learned to look into them and behind them. We have learned to read their language and fathom their depths of affection. Take away the spirit, and the face is nothing but a vacant and empty mask. So with the face of Jesus, we can only see His face when we have had communion with His spirit. A brilliant young Canadian artist, whose ambition it is to paint a great religious picture, has been making hundreds of draw-ings of the face of Christ from the great masters in an endeavour to find what is the peculiar spiritual quality of His face. Yet, I venture to suggest, that, if some day he does paint that picture, the Christ whom he will portray will not be the Christ whom he has seen upon the canvases of others, but the Christ whom he has come to know within his own heart, the Lord with whose spirit his soul has had fellowship.

It follows from this that though the actual face of our Saviour has been hidden from us in the wisdom of God, yet the reflection of His blessed face may still be seen in the faces of all who love Him and have communion with Him. There is such a thing as a Christ-like look, and those who walk most closely with the Lord "are changed into the same image from glory to glory." When the late C. F. Andrews arrived at the door of an English home where he was to stay as a guest, the servant girl who opened the door, rushed back to her mistress to tell her that Jesus Christ was at the door. The real likeness of the Son of Man is most surely reflected in the faces of those who possess His spirit and live in constant communion with Him. His true features are not to be seen so much on the canvasses in our picture galleries or in the images within our churches. They are to be seen wherever His disciples are busy about their Master's business.

But what can be said of the actual face of Jesus? This at least, that it was a human face, and like all true human faces which have not been frozen into rigid masks, it could and did reflect many moods; it mirrored many emotions. Because of the words of Isaiah in the fifty-third chapter of his prophecy, it has sometimes been assumed that there was nothing to attract

in the Master's countenance and we are asked to accept
as literal truth the claim that "He had no form nor
comeliness. . . . no beauty that we should desire him".[1]
That assumption seems hardly justifiable. At the
same time, under ordinary circumstances there does
not appear to have been anything outstandingly
attractive or appealing about His face. We read of no
artist seeking to draw those features; of no sculptor
being driven to perpetuate them in marble. His was
an ordinary human countenance, and here, as elsewhere, He chose to be one with us.

Yet, like every human face, His too was constantly
changing. With withering anger and scorn, it could
look upon Scribes and Pharisees and Temple usurers.
Little children were caressed by its tenderness. Anchor-
less multitudes felt at peace under the shadow of its
compassion. By the grave of Lazarus it was lined
with sorrow, wet with tears. At Gethsemane and on
Golgotha, it was convulsed and drawn with bitter
anguish. On Hermon and Olivet, it was transfigured
with a glory not of this earth. The face of Jesus
changed. The features remained the same but the form
was ever altering.

Those who looked upon Him, however, were never
in any doubt as to the spirit which was reflected there.
Always it was the spirit of perfect goodness and holy
love, the spirit of the Lord and Saviour of men. "What
is there in the face of Dante which is absent from the
face of Goethe?" Fitzgerald once asked of Tennyson.
"The Divine!" came the answer, and the Divine was
supreme in the face of Jesus of Nazareth. That was
why sinners shrank before His presence, clasped His
feet rather than look upon His face. That was why

[1] Isaiah 53:2.

pompous, self-righteous leaders hated Him. Their very hatred was an acknowledgement of His sovereign goodness, for before His face they found themselves self-condemned. At Horeb, we are told that "Moses hid his face; for he was afraid to look upon God."[1] And face to face with Jesus Christ, men knew the same terror, the same awful shame; for that face, human though it was, "reflected the light of the knowledge of the glory of God".

With what face, then, we may well ask, does Christ look upon us? Does He burn and wither us with the scorn of His anger, because like Scribes and Pharisees, like Simon the Leper or Caiaphas, we have made this holy religion which God meant to be a living recreating spirit into a dead ritual which condemns to misery those who should be free? Or does He look upon us with sorrowing compassion, as He did upon that Rich Young Ruler whose great possessions barred the way to life abundant? Or perhaps He looks upon us, even in the very hour of our prayers, with that hurt anger which once startled Peter because we too would have Him repudiate His Cross and smooth life's path for us into a silky way. Or I wonder if, perchance, He might look at any of us as He looked at Peter on that night in which He was betrayed,—looked across the darkness of the courtyard into the eyes of the man who had thrice denied Him? How does Christ look at us and with what gaze does He search our souls? It is a crucial question to which we have need to give an honest answer.

And in our heart of hearts, we know the answer; for there we stand condemned or acquitted, naked in guilt or clothed with righteousness. God be praised for the

[1] Exodus 3:6.

judgment of His presence! For the very look which the Lord turns upon us, confirms His love for us. His face may condemn our sins, but only because His heart cares for the sinner. It is only in the light of His countenance that we can find our peace; only in the sunshine of His face that we can find rest unto our souls.

> I looked to Jesus and I found
> In Him my Star, my Sun;
> And in that light of life I'll walk,
> Till travelling days are done.[1]

May the Lord, then, indeed "make His face shine upon us, and be gracious unto us: the Lord lift up his countenance upon us and give us peace."[2]

There is one further claim that we can make about our Saviour's face, this face that was human, yet reflected the Divine, this face which is veiled from our eyes, yet reincarnated in the faces of His followers. It is that someday, when the battle is over and the victory is won and we find ourselves standing at the last in His presence, then, if we have been faithful here, we shall be found to be like Him. St. Paul was in no doubt upon that point. Because on this earthly plane it is possible for us to reflect our Lord's glory, some day we shall "be changed into the same image from glory to glory".[3] St. John shared the same conviction. "We know that when He shall appear," he shouts in triumph, "we shall be like Him; for we shall see Him as He is."[4] Says Professor Gossip somewhere: "When

---

[1] Horatius Bonar, "I heard the voice of Jesus say".

[2] Numbers 6:24-26.

[3] II Corinthians 3:18.

[4] I John 3:2.

we get to heaven the angels will put their heads together and whisper, 'Look! See, how like the Lord he
is!   How like the Lord she is!' "

There can, of course, be no likeness to Christ unless
we keep looking at Christ. Those who live together in
love grow like each other, and to live with Christ in
love is to have constant communion with Him, the
communion of prayer and obedience and service. Thor-
walden in his most famous statue of our Lord has
vividly brought home this truth. There the Jesus of
"Come unto Me" stands a gracious figure with arms
outstretched to welcome all, but His head is lowered;
for, as its creator remarked, "If you want to see His
face, you must get on to your knees." Are we on our
knees often enough to be sure that we shall grow like
Him?

One of the lovely and touching stories that has
come to us from the pen of that famous Edinburgh
doctor, Dr. John Brown, concerns a ministerial friend
of his father who after two short years lost by death
his beautiful and deeply-loved wife. It was before the
day of the photographer's art, and the stricken husband had no portrait to comfort him in his grief.
Shortly after the funeral he purchased from an Edinburgh art store eight prepared ivories and the necessary
pigments, and with no previous training to guide him,
retired to the privacy of his study. For fourteen
days, he shut himself away from everyone, but at the
end of the time emerged ·haggard and weary but
triumphant, holding in his hand the one remaining
ivory on which was a most life-like likeness of his
beloved wife.[1]

It is only in the secret place, only by abiding under

[1] John Brown, *Horæ Subsecivæ.*

the shadow of the Almighty that you and I can ever hope to reproduce the divine likeness of that most wonderful of all faces. It was, you recall, while our Lord prayed that "the fashion of his countenance was altered",[1] and only on our knees can we ever hope to catch the reflection of the glory of God in the face of Jesus Christ. But there it can be reproduced, not on ivory, but on the indestructible canvas of our immortal spirits. There it will be made to live again in the lineaments of our souls. And one day when we do at last stand before His presence and see Him face to face, the angels will whisper together and say, "See, how like the Lord he is! How like the Lord she is!"

[1] St. Luke 9:29.

HIGHWAYS OF HIS HEART

VIII

THE WAY OF DISCIPLINE

And he came and dwelt in a city called Nazareth, that it might be fulfilled which was spoken by the prophets, He shall be called a Nazarene.

St. Matthew 2:23.

And they returned into Galilee, to their own city called Nazareth. And the child grew, and waxed strong in spirit, filled with wisdom; and the grace of God was upon Him.

St. Luke 2:39-40.

And he went down with them and came to Nazareth, and was subject unto them . . . And Jesus increased in wisdom and stature, and in favour with God and man.

St. Luke 2:51-52.

And Pilate wrote a title, and put it on the cross. And the writing was, *Jesus of Nazareth, the King of the Jews.*

St. John 19:19.

STRANGE, isn't it, that of all the great ones of the earth we know less about the major portion of our Lord's life than we do of almost any other! We know that He was born in Bethlehem of Judea, and while still an infant returned to Nazareth of Galilee. We know that for thirty years He lived there; but of all that happened to Him, of the experiences and adventures through which He passed, of the hardships and sorrows that weighed upon His spirit, of the joys and dreams, the hopes and fears that crowded and jostled each other within His heart, we know next to nothing!

73

What would we not give to know more of those "silent years"? How much it would mean, for example, to children and young people to know how Jesus spent His boyhood and youth and early manhood! Who would not wish to read of how He first learned to pray and of the prayer He offered; of the help He gave His mother about the home, and His growing skill at the trade of carpenter under the tutelage of Joseph; of those early struggles at school and adventures in the open air; of His thoughts and plans, His patience and passion for righteousness? A thousand things we crave to know, but the dark wall of silence remains impenetrable and unsurmountable. Into the lovely lines of a child's prayer Francis Thompson has put some of our restless questioning:

> Little Jesus, wast Thou shy
> Once, and just so small as I?
> And what did it feel like to be
> Out of Heaven, and just like me? . . .
> Hadst Thou ever any toys,
> Like us little girls and boys? . . .
> And did Thy Mother at the night
> Kiss Thee, and fold the clothes in right?
> And didst Thou feel quite good in bed,
> Kissed, and sweet, and Thy prayers said?[1]

We can ask the questions: the hard and well-nigh impossible thing is to find the answers.

At the same time, it is possible to exaggerate our ignorance with regard to those silent years. Wordsworth has reminded us that "The child is father to the man", and what Jesus was in His public ministry is the most eloquent witness of what He was becoming

[1] Francis Thompson, "Ex Ore Infantium". In *Selected Poems.* Burns, Oates & Washbourne Ltd. Courtesy Sir Francis Meynell.

during those long, quiet years among the "fair green
hills of Galilee that girdle quiet Nazareth".[1] Much
has no doubt been denied us, but by no means everything, and certainly not the essential things! Let us
try then to summarize the significance of those hidden
years at Nazareth. As we mark the way He travelled,
it may be that we too will discover a highway for our
hearts to pass along through the Nazareth to which
God in His loving wisdom has consigned us.

We do know, for example, that through childhood
and youth Jesus grew to mature manhood in one of
the good, if simple, homes of Nazareth. Whatever
His origins were in the beginning, there in Nazareth
He was known and acknowledged as the Carpenter's
Son, as Mary's Boy, and as such He was content to be
known. We know too that His parents, devout, God-
fearing people, supremely conscious of their great
responsibility, watched over Him lovingly, anxiously,
prayerfully with all a father's and mother's love and
care. Mary especially, like the mother of John Wesley, had a sense of destiny overshadowing her and her
son. Twice St. Luke refers to her mother's insight and
sensitiveness. At His birth "Mary kept all these
things and pondered them in her heart,"[2] and when
they returned from that memorable visit to Jerusalem
when He was twelve, "His mother kept all these sayings in her heart."[3] Long years afterwards, when His
work was finished and His kingdom had begun to come
in the hearts of men, she had told Luke himself of
those distant, dear days, and of how she had watched

[1] Eustace Rogers Conder: "Ye fair green hills of Galilee".

[2] St. Luke 2:19.

[3] St. Luke 2:51.

wonderingly within her own small kitchen this first-
born son of hers "increase in wisdom and stature, and
in favour with God and man".

Then again we know that in that home there were
brothers and sisters, and He who was first-born had to
play an elder brother's part in the lives of the younger
members of the family. It is not imagination but
knowledge that sees Him taking the hands of the baby
James and helping him take his first faltering steps.
It was He who shepherded the younger children to
the village school; who held them back from the
lumbering wheels of passing caravans or racing
chariots. It was He who ran errands for His mother,
drew water from the well, went searching for a lost
brother or sister, replenished the fire of a chilly evening, and did the thousand little things that train our
children in the ways of life. It was He too who put
strong arms about His mother and held her sobbing to
His breast that dark, desolate day when they laid the
good, wise, humble carpenter, Joseph, to rest in the
little God's acre up the hill. And it was He who so
selflessly stepped into Joseph's place as the mainstay
of that little home.

All this we know and know as fact, not fiction.
That is to say we know that through thirty years our
Lord subjected Himself to the discipline of homelife.
"He went down to Nazareth," says St. Luke "and was
subject unto them." Gladly He submitted to the
discipline of parental authority, and there in that poor
home, so poor indeed that the poorest of our homes
might very well look like a palace beside it, He learned
to live with other people, learned to submit to their
rule; acknowledged their authority; accepted their
judgments; adjusted Himself to their moods; and took

a full share of responsibility in all that concerned their wellbeing and happiness. In Nazareth Jesus proved Himself a true Son, a tried and trusted Elder Brother.

Can any of us hope to follow Christ faithfully, and yet not subject ourselves to this discipline? Can any attain to true Christian stature without submitting to the authority of home? There are many who rebel against this discipline, who despise the authority of their parents, who treat home with supercilious contempt, very sure that they are wiser than their fathers. Nevertheless the first of all laws of human conduct remains the ancient command: "Honour thy father and thy mother."[1] After the laws of religion, that is the most important of the laws of life. After our response to God, there is nothing so vital to our wellbeing as the response we give to the love of our parents.

Indeed, how can we ever be true children of God unless we begin by being faithful sons and daughters within our own homes? Home, to quote W. E. Channing, is "the nursery of the infinite". "Home interprets heaven," says another. "Home is heaven for beginners." Loyalty to home is the first loyalty of life, and submission to its discipline is the first step that any of us can take towards the fuller life of the sons and daughters of God. To be God's child, we must begin by proving ourselves faithful children of our earthly homes. That is the way our Lord took, and it remains the way of life for all who would follow Him.

Secondly, we know that in Nazareth Jesus followed his father's trade and became a carpenter. He subjected himself to the discipline of labour and submitted

[1] Exodus 20:12.

to the pressure of economic necessity. There, from under His hand, came cradles and coffins, symbols of the mysteries which surround our life. There, at His bench, He laboured making doors and windows, tables and chairs, yokes and ploughs, and, who knows, perhaps on occasion, under pressure from the military garrison, even a cross. By the labour of His hands, He earned a livelihood both for Himself and later for His widowed mother and fatherless brothers and sisters. Nazareth knew Him as the Carpenter. "Is not this the carpenter," they asked, "the son of Mary, the brother of James and Joses, and of Juda and Simon? And are not his sisters here with us?"[1] Nazareth knew Him as the mainstay of that little home.

As carpenter, our Lord also shared in the life of the community. Daily work brought Him close to the daily needs of His fellowmen, to their pains and problems, their moods and tempers, their sins and selfishness, their grandeur and greatness. He knew what it was to toil for little reward; knew the heartbreak of grinding poverty; knew the cruelty of sharp practice and greed for gain. In the sweat of His face did He eat bread.[2] Up there in Nazareth no stones were turned into bread, and many a time the wolf of hunger scraped and gnawed at the door of that little home. Jesus knew the tragedy underlying a poem, like Thomas Hood's "Song of the Shirt". He knew what Elizabeth Barrett Browning meant when she wrote the lines—

> The child's sob in the silence curses deeper
> Than the strong man in his wrath.[3]

[1] Mark 6:3.
[2] Genesis 3:19.
[3] E. B. Browning, "The Cry of the Children".

He knew that

> The path that leads to a loaf of bread
>   Winds through the swamps of toil,
> And the path that leads to a suit of clothes
>   Goes through a flowerless soil,
> And the paths that lead to the loaf of bread
> And the suit of clothes are hard to tread.[1]

Yet through it all, He was faithful, faithful though the dream in His heart was to go out and save the world; faithful as His brother James left home to join a strict religious sect, and His own dream faded into remoter distances; yes, faithful in all the little things until it was His Father's good pleasure to make Him ruler over many great things.

The Moravians in their litany offer the prayer: "May the precious sweat of Thy labour lighten our toil . . . May Thy faithfulness in Thy handicraft make us faithful in our share of labour."[2] How much we all need to offer that prayer! For one of the tragedies of Christendom is that we have not exalted labour as Christ did, and faithfulness in the work of our hands is not counted among us as virtue. One would have thought that the fact that His hands laboured would have exalted and consecrated all labour. But not so! Indeed multitudes live trying to escape from toil. Better to sit at a desk than stand at a bench, we think; or better still to be chained to neither desk nor bench! How many there are who sell their very souls to make money quickly in order that they may escape from the drudgery and discipline of a Nazareth of toil!

[1] Sam Walter Foss, "Paths".
[2] A. J. Gossip, in *The Speaker's Bible*, St. Luke Vol. I, James Hastings, ed.

How vain is such effort, for there is no escape from toil, not for anyone of us! "In the sweat of thy face shalt thou eat bread, till thou return unto the ground." "If any would not work, neither should he eat," says St. Paul,[1] for even the angels in heaven have to serve God. If then we would follow Christ, we must follow Him here and submit gladly to the discipline of labour. We must do with all our might what lies to our hands, and we must do it faithfully. For it is God Who has appointed us to our tasks. Every workman has a calling; every labourer is called of God. It was God Who appointed His Son to the carpenter's bench in Nazareth. It is God Who has placed us at the bench or desk or counter. The urge to do greater things may lie cradled in our hearts, but first we must serve in Nazareth; first we must prove faithful in the little things: and afterwards, if it is our Father's good pleasure, He will make us ruler over many things.

The discipline which Nazareth imposed upon our Lord however, is not complete without acknowledgement of the fact that there He submitted Himself to the discipline of the Church and its worship. The village synagogue was also the village school where the boy Jesus made His first acquaintance with the Bible of His people, committing much of it to memory, and learning to read it intelligently. Jesus had His own favourite copy of the Old Testament, specially thumbed and marked, and His own favourite books, in particular Deuteronomy and Hosea as well as the Psalter. We know too that He was regular in His attendance at the House of God, worshipping "as was His custom" every Sabbath Day along with His fellow

[1] II Thessalonians 3:10.

citizens. Further, we have it on Luke's authority, who got it from Mary herself, that from the age of twelve, He thought of God as "My Father" and of His business in life as "My Father's Business".

It is obvious from His later ministry that our Lord must have found much within the Church and its worship to weary and vex Him. He could not subscribe to so many crippling regulations and narrow-minded bigotries as crowded the religious life of His day. He hated the parade of righteousness made by religious leaders, and His whole soul rose in revolt against the claims of a special privilege and piety. Despite all this, however, He remained a true and faithful member of the Church, loyal and regular in His attendance at public worship. If later He criticized His Church and condemned some of its practices, He did so from within, not from without: He did so as one who had a stake in the ship and not as one who had abandoned it to destruction.

Here, too, there is much for us to learn from Christ's example. It is very easy to be critical of the Church, and rocket our criticisms upon it from without. But that was not the Master's way, nor is it the way His followers can take. Of course, there is much within the Church that is wrong, much that is a crying disgrace and scandal. Self-righteousness and Phariseeism are as virulent today as ever they were in Christ's time. The Church does not and indeed cannot read the signs of the time, nor does it hear the pitiful call of humanity for a Saviour. Instead we perpetuate our unholy divisions, cling to our antiquated methods, insulate ourselves from the living needs of men, and starve missionary enterprise by niggardly giving. It is significant that in this age of spiritual inertia we build government offices as cathedrals and churches as cellars! Sometimes I hate the Church and the parody of Christianity it presents. But I have a right to do so, for I have staked my life in its life; and that is the only ground from which Jesus would have His followers act.

It is high time that Christian people realized how all demanding are the claims of the Church, and how absolutely vital it is that we submit ourselves to its discipline and service, to its worship and work. The Church exists not for our enlightenment nor improvement, and certainly not for our amusement. It exists to be the living Body of Christ among men, the instrument of His salvation for the world. We who are its members are here not as connoisseurs but as crusaders, not as passengers but as pilgrims and pioneers. Only thus can the world be saved, and only thus can we ourselves wax strong in spirit and be filled with wisdom, and have the grace of God upon us.

"He went down and came unto Nazareth and was subject unto them." Two things happened in Nazareth. There God disciplined His Son for the ministry before Him. There the divine fitted into the framework of the human. There the holy Son of God became a humble man.

> My starry wings
> I do forsake,
> Love's highway of humility to take:
> Meekly I fit my stature to your need.[1]

But Nazareth also saw the human expanded until it could contain the divine; for Jesus also made the

[1] Evelyn Underhill: *Immanence*

life of Nazareth measure up to His divine standards and heavenly ideals. Up there man became God as well as God man, and it was the village Carpenter who built that bridge from earth to heaven so that we too can become the sons of God.

They called Him "Jesus of Nazareth" and it was as "Jesus of Nazareth" He died on Calvary. For first and last He was a man among men, a son and brother, a carpenter and citizen, a worker and worshipper. "We have not a high priest that cannot be touched with the feeling of our infirmities: but one that hath been in all points tempted like as we are, yet without sin."[1] For our High Priest was once "Jesus of Nazareth".

> And He loved Nazareth:
>   And so, I think, on Golgotha,
> When Jesus' eyes were closed in death,
>   He saw with love most passionate
> The village street at Nazareth.[2]

[1] Hebrews 4:15 (R.V.)
[2] Warburton Lewis: *Jesus of Galilee*. By permission of the author.

IX

THE WAY OF DEDICATION

Then cometh Jesus from Galilee to Jordan unto John
to be baptized of him. But John forbad him, saying,
I have need to be baptized of thee, and comest thou
to me? And Jesus answering, said unto him: Suffer
it to be so now: for thus it becometh us to fulfil all
righteousness.

St. Matthew 3:13-15.

My beloved Son, in whom I am well pleased.

St. Matthew 3:17.

Up in Nazareth for thirty long years our Lord subjected Himself to the way of discipline, the discipline
of love and labour and religion, of home and work and
Church. There He proved Himself a true son and
brother, a faithful workman and citizen, a loyal and
sincere communicant of His Church. Moreover He
persisted in this discipline while youth faded into manhood and manhood into maturity though the dream in
His heart was to go forth and "be about my Father's
business".[1]

At last, however, the way of discipline had its end.
The hard patient preparation of the Silent Years was
over and the way opened for Jesus to go forth and
fulfil His life's highest purpose. Jude and Simeon, His
two brothers, were now able to take over the carpenter's
business, while His sisters were already surrounding
Mary, His mother, with a loving watchful care. No
longer did the responsibilities of homelife bind Him to

[1] St. Luke 2:49.

His bench. So one day for the last time Jesus shook
the shavings from His tunic, handed over the shop to
His brothers, said a tender goodbye to His sisters,
kissed His mother and dried her tears, and then turned
His back upon Nazareth. Never again would He live
there as one of its citizens. The way of discipline was
over and ended.

His journey carried Him eastwards, down over the
brow of the hill, across the fertile plain of Esdraelon,
where the ripening barley waved in the fresh breeze,
until He reached the dark Gap of Jezreel. Plunging
into it He came down at last into the heats of Jordan.
Why did the Carpenter of Nazareth take this road, and
what destiny awaited Him by the Jordan's bank?

Our Lord's appearance at the river Jordan coin-
cided and was closely connected with the very remarkable ministry of John the Baptist. John was no
stranger to Jesus. Their mothers were close friends
and it is almost certain that the two sons had met
throughout the years, with each influencing the other.

For some time now John's ministry had proved
itself the most remarkable religious phenomenon
Palestine had witnessed in many generations. For the
first time in several centuries, men recognized in him
the authentic Voice of Prophecy, and a thrill of expectancy ran throughout the land at the very mention
of his name. "Was this the Messiah?" everyone was
asking. "Was this the long-looked-for Saviour of
Israel, the Promised One of God?" But there in the
wilderness skirting the Jordan valley, John had
preached with a new forthright fearlessness. He
attacked the religious corruptions of his day. He condemned those who put their trust in the privileges of

birth and background. To him the Pharisees and
Sadducees were a "brood of vipers", and he warned
them that God could raise up children to Abraham
from the very stones at their feet. Ruthlessly he attacked the evil practices of the so-called religious, and
demanded a new quality of life and a new attitude
towards God. Men must repent. There must be a
change of heart and a change of life, a new attitude
towards God and sin and your brother man. Let men
show their repentance in a new compassion for the
poor, a new scrupulousness in business dealings, a new
justice and honour. John had a word for everyone, for
soldiers and government officials, for priests and prel-
ates. His net was cast wide and it went deep. It
touched and troubled all classes, and brought multitudes to a place of new dedication and decision.

To Nazareth came a constant stream of reports
concerning John's ministry and message. In the
carpenter's shop they told of how a deputation from
Jerusalem had waited upon John to enquire if he were
the Messiah. The answer that he gave was that he
was no more than a Voice calling upon men to "prepare
the way of the Lord".[1]: He was certainly not the
Messiah. Nevertheless the Messiah was coming, and
the sign of His coming would be a baptism of fire
from above. So the cry echoed across the land:
"Repent! Repent! Repent! The Kingdom of Heaven
is at hand. Prepare the way of the Lord!" Little
wonder that He whose calling it was to be "about His
Father's business" turned His feet towards Jordan
when at last the discipline of Nazareth was ended.
Jesus made straight for John.

[1] St. Luke 3:4.

It was one of the great days of all time when Jesus arrived at Jordan and John recognized His friend in the crowd. Try to picture that meeting. Here is the strange wild man of the desert, rough, unshaven John, clad in a long camel's hair shirt, yet with eyes that flashed like living coals in that browned, weathered face, and before him stands Jesus, simply dressed like any countryman, and yet to John so different from any other who had ever sought his baptism. "John," says Jesus, "I have come to be baptized of you." And this man, this ruthlessly uncompromising prophet who has challenged and condemned princes and priests, who respects neither king nor commoner, starts back dumbfounded, nonplussed, unbelieving. "You, Jesus!" he says, "You want to be baptized by me! Why, it ought to be the other way round. It is I who should be baptized of you. I am not worthy to do this thing. I am not fit even to tie the laces of your sandals!" What a tribute that was to our Lord, coming as it did from such a fierce, fanatical prophet of righteousness! If John had had any doubts before as to who the Messiah was, those doubts vanished in that moment. He knew now that he was there in the presence of God's Chosen One! He knew that he was standing on holy ground!

But Jesus was insistent, and would brook no refusal. "Suffer it to be so now:" He commanded, "for thus it becometh us to fulfil all righteousness." So there in the eyes of all the people, He was baptized like any common sinner seeking forgiveness and confessing His need of newness of life. Why did Jesus insist on being baptized? Obviously John was convinced that He had no need of baptism. John was sure that Jesus was sinless and holy. Yet He insisted. Why?

The answer is that in baptism our Lord made a twofold dedication of Himself. On the one hand, He dedicated Himself utterly and absolutely to God and His service: on the other hand, He dedicated Himself to men and their salvation.

By this act of Baptism, Jesus openly and publicly dedicated Himself to God and to His service. He had no sin from which to seek remittance and cleansing, but He did have a life to give: and there in Jordan by the symbolism of immersion, He gave Himself utterly and without reserve to His Father in heaven. Throughout the years in Nazareth, the conviction had grown within His heart that He must serve God with all of heart and mind and soul and strength. His supreme calling must be to shew forth God to men and be God's messenger among men. So now when at last it was possible for Him to fulfil His calling, He began by an act of supreme dedication in baptism. There in the waters of Jordan, He died to all personal desire, will and ambition. He died to self and He lived to God, surrendering Himself unconditionally to do the will of His Father in heaven.

Can any of us, I wonder, ever hope to fulfil life's highest calling without just such an act of dedication? Living in God's world as God's children, how can we ever hope to fulfil His high purpose for us unless we commit our ways unto Him, and surrender our lives in a great act of consecration? Our fathers were wiser in these matters than we have been. They preached the need for conversion. They called for definite decisions. They insisted on dedication. They sang with fervour the words of a once familiar hymn,

> O happy day, that fixed my choice
> On Thee, my Saviour and my God![1]

They shouted with joy

> 'Tis done! the great transaction's done!
> I am my Lord's, and He is mine.[2]

When last did we sing that hymn with any meaning? Is the sad truth not that most of us have dedicated ourselves to anything and everything but to God and His service? Then we wonder why life should be so full of confusion and conflict!

Let me put in a plea, especially with those who are young, for a real dedication of ourselves and of our lives to God. Why go into your father's business, for example, just because it is the easy way? Or why set money-making as the "be all and end all" of our life's work? God's will for us is something that must be put above everything else, above home and self and society. His will for you may not be that you should become a brilliant surgeon, earning a thousand dollars for an operation; His will may be that as a foreign missionary you do that same operation for nothing somewhere in India or China. Or again His will for you may not be that you should live a life of quiet retirement, but rather that you step out into the arena of public life and play a great and noble part in shaping the destiny of your country and your world. "To choose your career for selfish reasons," said the late Archbishop of Canterbury, "is a worse sin than committing adultery,

---

[1] Philip Doddridge, "O happy day, that fixed my choice".
[2] Ibid.

for it is the withdrawal of the greater part of your time and energy from the service of God."[1]

If the little country from which I come has played a part out of all proportion to her size in the life of mankind, then I have no hesitation in attributing it to the consecration and dedication of generation after generation of men and women to the highest service of God. Year after year, men and women with the very highest qualifications that our schools and universities could give them have eschewed the temptations and profits of the world to go and teach and preach in little country schools and churches where God has used them to lay the foundations of a national life that cannot be shaken.

Is there anything more needed across the earth today than just such dedication? God is calling the young men and women of this generation, calling them to sacrifice all worldly gain and go out as ministers, teachers, doctors, nurses, into every part of this world. He offers them no ease, little leisure, few comforts. But He offers to use them in making a great nation, a great race whose life will stand foursquare on justice and truth, reverence and love. "Whom shall I send, and who will go for us?" comes the cry. Who will answer, as Isaiah did, as Christ did: "Here am I; send me"?[2]

Again, by going down into those waters of baptism, our Lord dedicated Himself to the service of His fellowmen. By this act, He who was sinless took His place at the side of sinners and submitted to the baptism of sinners. Ponder that fact well. Jesus from the very beginning of His public ministry refused to

[1] William Temple, *Christian Faith and Life.* Macmillan & Co. Ltd.

[2] Isaiah 6:8.

stand aloof, and insisted on identifying Himself utterly
with us. He placed Himself on the self-same level with
all mortals, and like the blackest sinner "fulfilled all
righteousness".

> O loving wisdom of our God!
>   When all was sin and shame,
> A second Adam to the fight
>   And to the rescue came.

> O wisest love! that flesh and blood,
>   Which did in Adam fail,
> Should strive afresh against their foe,
>   Should strive and should prevail.[1]

In his little book on the Life and Teaching of our
Lord, Professor J. S. Stewart points out that "the only
love which can ever possess redeeming power is a love
that goes all the way and identifies itself with others."[2]
He goes on to point out that it was such love which
made Moses pray on the day that Israel had sinned,
"Blot me out of Thy book of life which Thou hast written." It was that love which made St. Paul cry out, "I
could wish that myself were accursed from Christ for
my brethren, my kinsmen according to the flesh." It
was that love which made George Fox pray "to be baptized into a sense of all conditions, that I might know
the needs and feel the sorrows of all". And the same
love made Father Damien identify himself with his
lepers. "Whenever I preach to my people," he said, "I
do not say, 'my brethren', as you do, but 'we lepers'.
People pity me and think me unfortunate, but I think
myself the happiest of missionaries." And it was this

[1] John Henry Newman, "Praise to the Holiest in the Highest".

[2] J. S. Stewart, *The Life and Teachings of Jesus Christ*. Com-
mittee of Publications, Church of Scotland.

self-same love which Christ manifested when He went
down with John to be baptized in Jordan. For our
sakes and our salvation, He made Himself of no repu-
tation.

Again it is such love that is needed by each and all
who would seek to serve God in the service of their
fellowmen. For the greatest gifts that we can bring to
others, the greatest good we can do for our brothers
and sisters, are not things that we can legislate into
their lives, but only things that we can impart by
standing beside them, living with them, and pouring
out our love upon them. Much may be done by law,
but at the end of the day it is love that is the fulfilment
of the law; it is love that transcends and surpasses
law. What matters most in any nation are not its
statesmen nor its politicians, not its lawmakers nor
administrators, but the spirit of love and brotherhood
in the hearts of parents and teachers, of prophets and
preachers, of humble servants and saints. Against the
power of such love nothing can ever prevail.

I would ask you to mark the immediate consequences of Christ's dedication of Himself in Baptism.
There are four consequences specifically mentioned in
the Gospels.

In the first place, "the heavens were opened",[1] and
He who had dedicated Himself to God received a
clearer vision of God. Secondly, the Holy Spirit
descended upon Him. That is to say, Jesus received a
new endowment of power, a new vital sense of ability
to fulfil His divine mission among men. Then, thirdly
He was given a new consciousness of His own sonship.
A Voice, that to Him was none other than the Voice of

[1] St. Matthew 3:16.

God, sounded within His soul, saying, "This is my beloved Son."[1]   All through His life, Jesus had confessed that God was His Father: here in the hour of dedication, the Father acknowledges His Son.   Finally, the descent of the dove could only have had one meaning for our Master.   It meant sacrifice.   The dove is the only bird that was ever sacrificed in the Jewish Temple.   It was a symbol of sacrifice.   It spoke to Him of His own sacrifice for the sin of the world.   No wonder John seeing Jesus exclaimed, "Behold the Lamb of God, who taketh away the sin of the world."[2]

These consequences are no arbitrary happenings but the sure and certain fruit of our dedication to God and to His service among men.   Give yourself to Him, give yourself without let or hindrance, give to Him body, soul and spirit, and you too will see the heavens open in clearer spiritual vision.   You too will receive a new influx of power.   You too will discover that you are indeed the child of God, the well beloved son or daughter of the Most High, and gladly will you go forward to whatever sacrifice He may demand.

[1] St. Matthew 3:17.
[2] St. John 1:29.

X

THE WAY OF DECISION

Then was Jesus led up of the spirit into the wilderness to be tempted of the devil.

St. Matthew 4:1.

When our Lord stood at the side of John in the waters of Jordan, He made a twofold dedication of Himself. He consecrated Himself to God and His will and to man and his service. There with absolute abandon, He surrendered Himself to God, but He insisted upon doing so as an ordinary mortal standing by the side of sinners. The Lord of Glory made Himself known as the Son of Man. Furthermore this dedication was accepted and sealed by a threefold blessing which immediately followed His Baptism. There was granted to Jesus a clearer vision of spiritual realities, a new inflow of divine power, and a more profound consciousness of divine sonship. The Son of Man found Himself acknowledged as the Lord of Glory, the well-beloved Son of His Father. From that moment, He knew Himself as the Son of God whose mission in life was to be the Saviour of men.

But there can be no resting for anyone of us on this highway of life, and no sooner had Christ received these gifts and blessings than He found His feet being turned into a new and strange way, a path fraught with great perils, a highway of testing and trial and temptation, the way of decision.

Here, then, is the first thing that challenges our attention, the startling fact that our Lord's temptation was the direct consequence of His consecration and dedication in Baptism. "Jesus," says St. Luke, who echoes the other evangelists, "being full of the Holy Ghost returned from Jordan, and was led by the spirit into the wilderness, being forty days tempted of the devil."[1] It was not the devil that drove Him into the wilderness, but the Spirit of God which had taken possession of Him in Jordan, the spirit that was aflame within His soul.

We are face to face here with a law of all spiritual life and growth, the simple principle that dedication demands decision; that consecration calls for choice and choice necessitates conflict. It is obvious, of course, that the higher anyone climbs, the greater is the danger of a fall. The nearer a soul approaches to God, the deeper is hell. But it is also true that having committed ourselves to God and His will, there immediately arises the problem of interpreting God's will in daily life. Dedication must be translated into deeds, and that immediately raises difficulties. It immediately gives the devil his chance to tempt and torture our souls. Notice too that the choice before us is not just a simple choice between good and evil. Very often it is much more subtle than that, and in Christ's own case it was certainly a choice between the good and the better, between the better and the best.

The New Testament is full of illustrations of this fact. The account of the temptation which we have here is only the first of a series of temptations which Jesus had to face. St. Luke makes that clear. "When the devil had ended all the temptation, he departed from Him for a season."[2] But it was not long before

[1] St. Luke 4:1-2.
[2] St. Luke 4:13.

he was back. He was there tempting our Lord when
the religious leaders came asking for a sign from
heaven. He was there in the guise of friend and
disciple that day at Caesarea Philippi when Peter
rebuked Him for suggesting that the Messiah would
ever have to die on a cross. He was there again in the
deep darkness of Gethsemane and even as He hung
on Calvary the hot breath of the tempter fanned His
cheek. "If He be the King of Israel, let him now come
down from the Cross, and we will believe him."[1] Every
great spiritual experience of His life had to be secured
and sealed by spiritual conflict, by agony of soul and
the torment of temptation.

To follow Christ, then, does not mean any easy
escape from temptation, but an intensification of
temptation. So often we delude ourselves by picturing
the Christian Life as a blessed lotus land where the
soul escapes from all evil and effort. Nothing could be
further from the truth. It is the pagan worldling who
is tempted least, the sinners not the saints! It is the
good, not the bad, who must walk through these flames
and be scorched by them. One has only to glance
casually through the great literature of devotion to
realize this fact. Read Augustine's *Confessions* or
Thomas A. Kempis' *Of the Imitation of Christ;* listen
to Bishop Andrewes or William Law or Alexander
Whyte at prayer, and none will be left in any doubt as
to the reality and power of temptation in the lives of
the saints of God. Each and all of them found life a
battle, a constant warfare against the hidden powers
of darkness. But they also found that in that conflict
they won their crown and earned the right to enter in

[1] St. Matthew 27:42.

and possess new territories of the soul. You remember
Bishop Blougram's words in Browning's poem:

> When the fight begins within himself,
> A man's worth something. God stoops o'er his head,
> Satan looks up between his feet—both tug—
> He's left, himself, i' the middle: the soul wakes
> And grows. Prolong that battle through his life!
> Never leave growing till the life to come![1]

It was the Spirit of God, then, not the devil that
drove our Master into the wilderness of temptation.
His new sense of power, His new conviction of sonship,
His new consciousness of a mission in life, all demanded
a new estimate of life, a new approach to living, a new
plan of action. Thus the way of temptation became
for Him the way of decision. We are surely wrong to
think of this mortal struggle as being a negative thing,
a matter only of resisting evil. In actual fact its
greatest consequences are always positive. For temptation faced and overcome always means a plan and
policy for the future, a new highway for our hearts
across life's uncharted continent.

Turn now to the actual temptations which our Lord
had to face during those six weeks spent in that fierce,
terrible wilderness of rock and ravine which hems in
the Jordan valley. Jesus Himself must have been the
source from which the evangelists derived their account
of that experience, for during those weeks He was completely alone, with none but God and the wild beasts
to see Him. "Every word," says Principal Curtis, "tense
and pregnant with meaning, betrays His profound

[1] Robert Browning: "Bishop Blougram's Apology".

and searching thought and His manner of speech."[1]
Indeed, the more one studies these three temptations,
the more tremendous they appear. "You cannot have
a storm in a wayside pool," someone has said. "The
typhoon needs the spacious sky, and the sweep of the
sea. The extent of the storm depends upon the capacity
presented." And the capacity presented here was that
of all heaven and earth and hell. None but the Son of
God could have been tried and tested in this way.

It is of course impossible in this brief compass to
do anything like justice to these three temptations of
which our Lord has told us. Let us concentrate attention then upon one particular characteristic common
to all these temptations, and which has a special
relevance for us. It is that our Lord was not tempted
at the points of weakness within His life but at the
points of strength. His greatest temptations centred
round His divine sonship, His religious convictions,
His possession of power and His passionate love for
men. Moreover it is at these very points that we and
with us all mankind are most severely tried and tested
throughout our lives. The danger point for all of us
is not the human but the divine in life, not the physical
nor material but what Addison calls "the divinity that
stirs within us."[2]

*In the first place, it was as the Son of God that
Jesus was supremely tempted and not as Mary's Son.*
This temptation was twofold in its thrust, for on the
one hand He was tempted to doubt his divine sonship
and on the other to presume upon that sonship. "Thou
art my beloved Son in whom I am well pleased."

[1] W. A. Curtis, *Jesus Christ the Teacher*. Oxford University
Press.

[2] Joseph Addison, *The Campaign*. v.i.7.

Those words were ringing in His ears as He made His way into the wilderness, but after weeks of fasting and loneliness when physical strength ebbed and spiritual vitality was consumed by thought, there came the temptation to doubt; and the devil saw his chance. "If thou be the Son of God" he kept repeating to Him. Yes, if you are indeed God's Son, then why hunger? Why be bound by economic laws and physical limitations? Why not turn stones into bread and claim the protection of the angels in heaven? Why sit silent and alone when the universe is yours and the kingdoms of this earth can become kingdoms of the Son of God? In each case Jesus was tempted either to doubt His divine sonship or presume upon that sonship and claim privileges denied to ordinary mortals. Yet in each case He rejected the tempter. He would not make a spiritual relationship to be bound by material events. As a true obedient Son He refused to force His Father's hand by demanding a sign or claiming a privilege. Instead, with simple faith and loving trust, He humbled Himself under the mighty hand of God.

But is it not just here that the greatest temptations of our lives lay hold upon us? We too are the sons of God. Yet how often there comes the temptation either to doubt our sonship, or presume upon that sonship? When John McNeil, the evangelist, went on one occasion to visit a dying man, he was summarily dismissed. "When I die, I'll die like a dog," he was told and there are many people who certainly live like that. They live despising their sonship and degrading their manhood. They debase the divine to the level of the animal. They are quite sure that when they die they will die like dogs.

But over against this is the temptation to accept

our divine sonship and presume upon it. Many people live secretly hoping that God will show them special favour. He will give them both bread and cake. He will protect their going out and coming in and send His angels to have charge over them. As His children, these things are regarded as rights, and claimed as the rewards for virtue. Yet He who was God incarnate never made such claims, never asked for such rewards. Instead He accepted hunger and loneliness, weakness and suffering, sorrow and death as His portion. He, who claimed to be the only Begotten Son, also put Himself utterly at the mercy of God's holy will so that at the last He was able to accept the cross of shame and find in it the path to glory. A true son will honour and obey his father. He will trust and love his father. He will never compel nor coerce his father. Let us, who are God's children, remember that. Let us follow Jesus the perfect Son.

Secondly, it was as a devout Believer and faithful Member of His Church that our Lord was tempted, and tempted out of the very Book that claimed to interpret God's will to Him. At baptism, God had spoken to His Son. It was natural therefore that the Son should turn to His Bible, the written Word of God, to discover from its pages how the Son of God should act among men. But when Jesus looked into His Old Testament, He discovered that it spoke not with one voice but with two voices. Large portions of Scripture supported the view that the Messiah should turn stones into bread, should expect special consideration and protection from the angels in heaven, and should establish a vast world-wide kingdom among men. Nor was the devil slow to remind Him of this. He quoted Scripture and he quoted it well.

On the other hand, there were portions of Scripture which depicted the Messiah's role very differently. His kingdom was to be spiritual not temporal, a kingdom within the hearts, minds, consciences of men rather than outward and earthly. Above all He was to identify Himself with sinners, saving them by His own sacrifice rather than wading through blood to a throne. Between these two voices Jesus had to choose, and again He chose the higher, the more spiritual and sublime and selfless conception in place of the more material view so popular among men of His own day.

To no man does religion speak with one voice, and one voice only. It speaks with many voices. To some it preaches a doctrine of narrow prejudice, of legal demands, of obedience to every jot and tittle of the law, and of persecution for those who are not of our particular persuasion. To others it speaks the language of a broad compassion and a deep love for all men; it proclaims a gospel of brotherhood, a ministry of mercy. Again to some its main concern must always be with this life and this world, with material blessings and temporal gifts, with a social gospel; for religion's main business, they argue, is with the here-and-now. But for others its primary message is to the heart and mind and conscience. Its kingdom is within; its conquest is unseen; its crown and country lie far beyond reach of time and space, of sense and sight.

Religion speaks with many voices, and it is no easy thing to decide which voice is the highest, which word is the word of God. But our Lord has given us His example to follow, and none can go far wrong, if, like Him, we give ear to the still small Voice of the Spirit, and in everything set our affections on things which are above and lay up treasures in heaven where neither moth nor rust corrupt. The highest religion is always the most spiritual religion.

Thirdly, our Lord was tempted in the wilderness at the point of His new-found Power. Power had been given to Him there in Jordan, undreamed of power. But how was He to use it? Was He to turn it towards alleviation of this life's physical and material handicaps? Was He to use it to feed and clothe, to heal and help the unhappy children of His day and generation? Or must He harness it only to spiritual purposes, and make it the minister of divine love and mercy? We know well the choice which He made there.

Is there anything in this world more dangerous or difficult to use aright than power? Certainly nothing has brought more misery upon the earth than the misuse of power, the corruption of power, the harnessing of power to material ends and carnal desires. Power we have, power unlimited,—power of thought and of action, of invention and creation. Harnessed to the chariot of Mars it has made a very successful effort to blow up and finally destroy the civilization of many centuries. Twice within our lifetime it has run amok, and plunged the world into bloody war. Today too, our statesmen and rulers, our warriors and workers dream of harnessing it to the shafts of a new world order, but it is primarily a material order, an order of better housing, better wages, better amusements. But can man live by bread alone? Can all the material prosperity in the world ever guarantee the things we need most, peace and joy and a quiet heart? A man may gain the whole world and lose his own soul, and what then shall it profit him? Beware of the use you make of your power! Let the Church and the Nation beware, for so many of our fair dreams for tomorrow are in imminent danger of once more being wrecked because we seek to use it as the devil wants us to use it and not as Christ has shown us how it ought to be used.

Finally, there in the wilderness our Lord was tempted at the point of His deep passionate love for men. How great must have been the temptation to begin His ministry by sweeping away those crushing, crippling economic hindrances which were breaking the hearts and bowing the backs of millions of his fellows! How he longed to have men follow Him and believe in Him, as they would do if He would work some stupendous miracle! In a world of corrupt leadership, how He craved to take the government upon His shoulders and by sweeping away the wrongs establish an outward, earthly kingdom of righteousness! But once again He refused, for man is not made for time but for eternity, and the salvation of his body is a very little thing compared to the salvation of his immortal soul.

The salvation of his body is a very little thing compared in importance with the salvation of his immortal soul. Do we remember this? Do our would-be reformers remember it? Do you and I who have homes and loved ones and children depending upon us, remember it? "Man's chief end is to glorify God and enjoy Him for ever."[1] But how many of us make that our life's chief end? How many of us "seek first the kingdom of God and His righteousness"? How many of us lay up for ourselves and for those we love treasure in heaven where neither moth nor rust corrupt, where

[1] *The Shorter Catechism.* Question 1.

XI

THE WAY OF CONSECRATION

And it came to pass about an eight days after these
sayings, He took Peter and John and James, and
went up into a mountain to pray. And as He prayed,
the fashion of His countenance was altered. . . .

St. Luke 9:28-29.

(Cf. St. Matt. 17:1-9; St. Mark 9:2-10; St. John 12:23-41;
II Peter 1:16-18).

FEW EVENTS in our Lord's life are at once so familiar
and so baffling as His Transfiguration. The story is
familiar, for all three evangelists record it, with St.
Luke giving the fullest account. In comparing his
record with the other two, one gets the impression that
with his acute historical sense, he had carefully checked
over each detail; and certainly his record adds con-
siderably to our knowledge of what actually happened
there on the mount.

According to Luke, it was "about eight days" (not
six as the others tell us) after the Great Confession,
that Jesus accompanied by the inner circle of the
disciples, Peter, James and John, withdrew "into a
mountain to pray".[1] Prayer was the primary reason
for our Lord's retreat, while the mountain to which He
withdrew was almost certainly Mount Hermon, that
noble peak rising over nine thousand feet high just
north of Galilee and source of the river Jordan.
Caesarea Philippi, scene of Peter's glorious confession
lay in the valley immediately to the south, while there

[1] St. Luke 9:28.

on the slopes of Hermon, Heaven itself confirmed that faith in Jesus already expressed by mortal man.

It was probably evening when the Master led His disciples up the mountain-side to the place of prayer, and through the long darkness of the night He wrestled in prayer, while the disciples slept.   Then towards morning He was transfigured.   Whatever actually happened, we do know that "as He prayed, the fashion of His countenance was altered, and His raiment was white and glistering", "exceeding white", says Mark who echoes St. Peter, "so that no fuller on earth could whiten them."[1]   To the fearful amazement of the disciples, they saw two men talking with Him, Moses and Elijah.   They also were enfolded in the splendour of light.   They "appeared in glory" says Luke, "and spake of His decease (His exodus) which He should accomplish at Jerusalem."   "Master," suggested Peter, like a man in a dream, "it is good for us to be here: let us make three tents, one for You and one for Moses and one for Elijah!"[2]   How like Peter—practical, forthright Peter, always wanting to be doing something! Here he is proposing to build a tent for Moses, a shelter for Elijah, and both of them many centuries dead!

The words were hardly out of his mouth when Another drew near.   A cloud overshadowed the mountain as centuries before a cloud had overshadowed Sinai and Carmel, and out of the thick darkness a Voice spoke, as once before it had spoken to Moses and Elijah and Jesus.   "This is my beloved Son: hear Him."[3] Wild terror laid hold upon the disciples and froze them to the ground.   Matthew tells us that a hand touched

[1] St. Mark 9:3.

[2] St. Luke 9:31-33.

[3] St. Mark 9:7.

them. The hand of Jesus was upon them and there was comfort and quiet in His voice: "Arise, be not afraid." "And looking up they saw no one save Jesus only."[1]

There is the story, told with such simplicity and sincerity by each of the evangelists that there can be no doubting its truth. "The narratives," says Principal Martin, "throw upon the mind of the reader the most powerful sense of the reality of the event."[2] Here is what happened, but how can we hope to understand it?

We can never fathom fully the mystery of this extra-ordinary incident: and for this reason that its primary purpose was not to quicken the disciples' faith but to strengthen our Lord's consecration of Himself. Jesus was the main actor and benefactor; the disciples were spectators. Moreover, "the fact to which the narrators point transcends experience, and imagination can create nothing which transcends experience." Principal Martin points this out, and he continues, "Here we have no dream of a fevered twilight, but the fit expression of a mystery, beyond thought and observation, of insight and vision, where the soul is like a dreamer, enthralled by sleep, and struggling with all his might to make some familiar motion."[3] The world beyond the grave is here on the mount, and of that world you and I know nothing, can know nothing, because we are still imprisoned within the womb of our mortality.

Nevertheless these accounts of the Transfiguration have not been preserved simply to baffle and confuse.

[1] St. Matthew 17:7-8.

[2] Hasting's *Dictionary of Christ & the Gospels*. "Transfiguration", Principal A. S. Martin, p. 743. Charles Scribner's Sons.

[3] Ibid, p. 744.

There is a message here for us as there was for Christ and primarily it is a message for us about Christ.

In thinking about the Transfiguration it is all-important to remember that it followed almost immediately upon Peter's Great Confession: "Thou art the Christ, the Son of the Living God."[1] On that occasion Jesus had pointedly asked His followers who they thought He was. Already His own mind was clear. He knew Himself to be the Messiah, the chosen One of God and that day at Caesarea Philippi His disciples also acknowledged His divine kinship. But there was this difference: their view of the Messiah's office was in direct conflict with His own view. To these men the Messiah must come as a sovereign and conquering King and Lord. So when Jesus spoke of going to Jerusalem to "suffer many things of the elders and chief priests and scribes, and be killed", it sounded to them like a terrible travesty, a sacrilege. This was not the Messiah of popular faith! Yet it was such a Messiah that Jesus had chosen to be, and chosen long ago as He wrestled with the Tempter in the wilderness.

Might it not well be then that this recoil of the disciples from the picture of a suffering and dying Christ compelled our Lord once more to question His own conviction? Once more He found Himself examining the very basis of His faith and life. Thus in search of light, in search of divine confirmation, He withdrew up the mountain to pray, and as He prayed confirmation came in the ravishing glory of the Transfiguration. And what confirmation it was!

In the first place, Moses and Elijah drew near and

[1] St. Matthew 16:16.

talked with Him of "His decease which He should accomplish at Jerusalem". Why Moses and Elijah? There are, I would suggest, three reasons for their presence there on the Mount with Jesus.

First, they came to comfort and strengthen Him in the loneliness of that hour. Madeline Rock has a little poem in which she describes our Lord as, "The Lonely Greatness of the World". No one was ever more alone than Jesus. Yet there were others who had also stood alone as they fulfilled God's high calling and none more so than Moses and Elijah. Says one writer, "we should not think of Moses and Elijah merely as conspicuous Old Testament figures, but as supremely solitary men, whose courage though strained almost to breaking point, had carried them through, and who for this reason were able to do service in His need to the Son of man."

There is profound truth here. Did not Moses stand alone mediating between a foolish, ignorant and carnally-minded Israel and God? Had he not pled for them offering his own life if only God would spare them? And at last it was this man who died utterly alone on Pisgah. And then Elijah. Alone he had defied the idolatrous priests of Baal. Alone he had challenged King and Commoner, Church and State armed only with simple passionate faith in God and at the last he too passed out alone on his chariot of fire into that larger realm that lies on the other side of death. The presence of these two great men who had themselves lived such lonely lives must have strengthened and confirmed and reassured our Lord as He turned His face to the unutterable loneliness of the Cross.

Secondly, they came to confirm His own faith, His

deep messianic convictions. If three of the loneliest of the sons of men met that day on Hermon, three who had climbed the highest mountains of the spirit also met. The man of Sinai and the man of Carmel held converse with Him who on another mount had claimed that He had come to "fulfil the law and the prophets".

It was our Lord's claim that He had come to write a new law upon the tables of men's hearts. He had come to lead them along a new highway of the Spirit unknown to the prophets of old. But was He right? In His inmost soul He believed that He was and now in the glory of the transfiguration Moses came to confirm His reading of the law and Elijah to support His interpretation of the prophets. They knew now, what they had not known while on earth, that it was for this Jesus and for the fulfilment of His life and teaching that they had lived and suffered and died. So they talked with Him of His exodus. They confirmed Him in His faith. They acknowledged Him to be the chief cornerstone of the arch, the foundation of whose pillars they had laid in the law and the prophets. Here on Hermon, the old Revelation finds its perfect fulfilment in the new Life "full of grace and truth".

A third reason for the presence of Moses and Elijah on the Mount of Transfiguration has been suggested by Warburton Lewis in his great book, *Jesus of Galilee*. In a fine chapter on the Transfiguration, Mr. Lewis argues that our Lord, who had been questioning the character of His Messiahship, not only received confirmation from these two Old Testament leaders, but they brought Him the further assurance that even now the Gate of Heaven was open to welcome Him home, if He would but go with them. These two whose graves have never been found upon the earth, who were trans-

ported and transfigured into glory, had come to tell
Him that He had not lived in vain. In very truth He
had walked before God with a perfect heart. They told
Him, says Lewis, that "the courts of Heaven were
hushed to welcome Him; the harps were strung to the
anthem that should burst from them all when at last
the Conqueror stepped into their midst."[1] Already
Jesus had won His way out of all mortal weakness and
sinfulness and ambition. "By the sheer clear right of
His holy living" He had gained for Himself "a passage
into Paradise." And that day on the mount they told
Him so. For Him there was no need to die. The Gate
of Heaven stood wide open to receive Him. The harps
of Heaven were "hushed only to crash in welcome as
His flaming feet passed the door."[2]

There was no need for Christ to die, and from Hermon He might well have ascended and passed for ever
from our ken. But we know that He did not accept
their offer to convoy Him in through the gates of
Paradise. Instead He spoke to them of Jerusalem, of
suffering, and death, and shame outside a city wall,
not of glory. Instead He dismissed Moses and Elijah.
He renounced heaven for Himself. He chose hatred
and gall, agony and death, and He did so because He
would not go there without us.

On Hermon, as at His Baptism, as at His temptation, He identified Himself completely and utterly
with the children of men. Because He knew that
without Him none of us could ever hope to win to
Heaven's gate, He put off His transfigured robes; He
turned His back upon glory; and once more accepted

[1] F. Warburton Lewis, *Jesus of Galilee*. By permission of the
author.

[2] Ibid.

the garments of shame and mockery, of dishonour and death, that He might bind Himself to us by bonds that can never be broken. And so as Moses and Elijah vanish from sight, and a great cloud sweeps down upon the mountain, a new Christ comes back to us, a greater Christ, our Christ, our Saviour, One with us forever.

But He was also now the Christ of God in a new way, for when the glory had passed; when He was clad once more in the simple homespun of a Galilean peasant; when the clouds rolled down the mountain and the vision was lost; when He had taken death as His portion, the Cross as His reward, then came the greatest confirmation of all. Then and only then the silence of heaven was broken and once more mortal man heard the Voice of the Immortal God: "This is my beloved Son; hear Him." A week ago mortal men had proclaimed Him, "The Son of God". Today the Immortal God acclaims Him, "My Beloved Son", beloved because He loved us and gave Himself for us; beloved because He fulfilled to the last God's holy redeeming purpose for our race. It is such a God who sits upon the throne forever.

> All hail, Redeemer, hail!
> For Thou hast died for me:
> Thy praise shall never, never fail
> Throughout eternity.

"And looking up they saw no one save Jesus only." There is no God in this universe other than the God and Father of our Lord Jesus Christ.

XII

THE WAY OF COMMUNION

(Christ) who in the days of his flesh, when he had offered up prayers and supplications with strong crying and tears unto him that was able to save him from death, and was heard for his piety . . . became the author of eternal salvation unto all of them that obey him.

Hebrews 5:7-9.

A tremendous subject is opened by these words, for they carry us into the Holy of Holies within our Lord's life. They take us along the greatest of all the Highways of His Heart, the highway of prayer, the way of His communion and fellowship with God. Jesus was not only a man disciplined and dedicated, tempted and transfigured; He was also a man of prayer, and that path, more than any other, was worn smooth by the constant passage of His feet upon it. Within the New Testament, there are at least fifteen specific references to Jesus at prayer, along with a considerable body of His teaching about prayer. In the brief compass of this chapter one cannot possibly do justice to so much material, far less to so great a subject. Our attention must therefore, be confined to one or two of the outstanding features which emerge as supremely significant from the Master's life of prayer.

In the very forefront, there is the place which He gave to prayer within His own life. Our Lord put prayer in the first place among all His duties and responsibilities. He gave prayer a pre-eminence over everything else, and to the end it remained the most important task that He had to do.

That is something to think over. Let us ask what is the most important thing that we have to do, what takes precedence in our lives. My own personal answer would not be that prayer comes first and how many others would have to make a similar confession? In few lives does prayer take precedence over everything else. But not so with Jesus. With Him the order was always prayer first: prayer before preaching; prayer before healing the sick or raising the dead; prayer before training the disciples; prayer before food and sleep and relaxation!

The lives of the apostles and saints confirm this order, for there is nothing in which they have more faithfully followed our Lord than in giving prayer precedence over everything else in life. St. Paul did that, and his epistles are full of appeals to his readers to pray, and "pray without ceasing", and to remember him and his work in prayer. It was the same with Martin Luther, who regarded prayer as the Christian's real trade or calling. "As a shoemaker makes a shoe, and a tailor makes a coat," he used to say, "so ought a Christian to pray. Prayer is the daily business of a Christian." One might well cross the centuries and span the continents culling instance after instance of the pre-eminence given to prayer by Christ's followers. Yet we so often put prayer down at the end of the list, among the fag ends of our life's tasks!

Andrew Bonar, the hymn writer, when speaking of his crowded ministry in a large Glasgow congregation, confessed to having failed as we have failed. "I was living very grossly," he wrote, "labouring night and

day in visiting, very little prayerfulness. I did not
see that prayer should be the main business of every
day." But Bonar did eventually see. "Unless I get
up to the measure of at least two hours in pure prayer
every day, I shall not be satisfied,"[1] he vowed, and his
friends noted the change, for in his ministry more
prayer meant more effectiveness. "He descended upon
his work," wrote Sir William Robertson Nicoll after his
death, "and so, while unresting, he was unhasting.
There was a kind of still brightness about him when
he visited. The work did not seem irksome; he did
not need to watch for opportunities of spiritual converse; everything came naturally; his labours did not
exhaust him and the edge remained on his spirit."[2] If
only Christian people knew what they were missing of
peace and poise and power through neglect of prayer,
nothing could keep them back from making it "the
main business of every day"!

Neglect of prayer is almost always due to one
thing, namely failure to realize our utter dependence
upon God. It is so easy to think of oneself as self-
sufficient and to stand alone, trusting in neither God
nor man, but only in ourselves. Jesus never did that,
nor have the saints and martyrs ever done that! One
and all lived supremely conscious of their utter
dependence upon God. In Him they lived and moved
and had their being. Not a breath of their bodies, not
a thought of their minds, not an impulse of their spirits
would they claim as their own apart from God. And
that sense of absolute dependence upon Him sent them
to their knees in daily prayer. They cast all their care

[1] William R. Nicoll, *Princes of the Church*. Hodder &
Stoughton Ltd.

[2] W. R. Nicoll, Op. cit.

upon Him who cared for them, with the result that they were ultimately able to stand among men independent, the masters, never the slaves, of circumstance, the creators of new worlds not merely the creatures of an old world.

Jesus put prayer first in His life because nothing could have any meaning for Him apart from God. He humbled himself under the mighty hand of God, and in due season God exalted Him, as He will exalt all who will seek first His Kingdom and Will along this narrow path of prayer.

A second outstanding fact about our Lord's prayer life was that every time of crisis found Him on His knees. Each new decision or fresh departure in His ministry, each hour of temptation or trial was approached by Him through prayer.

It was while praying in the waters of the Jordan that "the heaven was opened and the Holy Ghost descended" upon Him.[1] The night, before He chose the twelve disciples, was spent in prayer. Prayer preceded Peter's "Great Confession", and some days later while He prayed "the fashion of His countenance was altered" and He was transfigured.[2] Jesus prayed in the Upper Room, and, later that same night, Gethsemane witnessed His bitter agony of blood and tears, "the highest moment in the history of prayer",[3] it has been called. Finally, three of the seven words spoken as He died upon the Cross were prayers: the first, a prayer for those who crucified Him, "Father, forgive them; for they know not what they do";[4] the second,

[1] St. Luke 3:21.
[2] St. Luke 9:29.
[3] Professor Hoffding, quoted by F. Heiler, in *Prayer*.
[4] St. Luke 23:34.

the terrible cry of dereliction, "My God, my God, why hast Thou forsaken me";[1] and the last, a triumphal surrender, "Father, into Thy hands I commend my spirit."[2]

Jesus met every crisis of His life girt about by prayer. Never once did He go down into the arena of temptation or pass through the searing, scorching fires of suffering without first putting His own hand firmly into the Hand of His Father. And notice more particularly that in almost every instance, His prayers preceded the crisis. Through prayer He prepared Himself to meet and master life's most testing experiences.

If few of us make prayer "the main business of every day", most of us are like our Master in that we turn to God in the crises of life. The unfortunate thing, however, is that, since prayer holds such a secondary place within our lives, we too often put off turning to God until the storm has already broken and the danger is imminent. We pray, but not until the doctor has given his disturbing verdict; not until the war cannot be avoided; not until the battle is actually raging; not until the fury of temptation has engulfed us; not until the sorrows of death have hold upon us. We pray but in desperation and despair, like a drowning man clutching at a straw. Can one wonder if such prayers are no more than broken, agonized cries, distress signals rather than the communion of the Christian with his God?

It was so different with Jesus. He used prayer like a wise general choosing his ground carefully for the forthcoming battle. He used it to make sure before the conflict began that His lines of communication

[1] St. Matthew 27:46.
[2] St. Luke 23:46.

would remain open and His supplies of spiritual grace and strength prove adequate for every emergency. The result was that the real victories of His life were victories won in prayer. Because He prayed before the crises, He conquered in the crises; because He agonized in Gethsemane, He triumphed on Golgotha. Always prayer meant for Jesus a strengthening of faith, a confirmation of His purposes, a new quietness and confidence, a fresh inflow of spiritual grace and power. When the storms did break around Him, He had already won through to the peace at their centre. His feet were firm on a rock, and His soul had found a hiding place from the storm and a covert from the tempest.

Here, then, is another reason why prayer should be the daily business of our lives; for only those who are constant in prayer can use it aright in the day of ordeal. Only those who pray earnestly and regularly can pray vitally and victoriously when the battle is on and the enemy is advancing against us. On one occasion Oliver Cromwell while examining the statues of some of his famous predecessors, turned to a friend with the remark: "Make mine kneeling for thus I came to glory."[1] It was kneeling that Jesus came to His Kingdom. It is only kneeling that any one of us can win through to the life victorious and everlasting.

A third characteristic of our Lord's prayer life was that first and last it was the highway of His communion with God. To Jesus God was real; God was living; God was near. Prayer was no mere performance of a religious ritual, but something so wonderful and intimate that earthly friendship and love paled

[1] David Williamson, *Gathered Harvest*. Rich & Cowan.

beside it. It came first in His life because of all experiences none could compare with it for reward and blessing.

He called God "Father" because He knew Him as Father, an all-loving and ever-present Father, Who was vitally interested in every detail of His life; Who was ready to help Him at every turn of the road; Who was certain at the last to bring Him home to glory. Because of this, thanksgiving filled His prayers, and praises flowed from His lips. Whenever a new joy came His way, or a new encouragement braced His spirit, or a new hope kindled its beacon across the night of His sky, Jesus had to go and tell His Father about it. He had to pour out His praise and thanksgivings in prayer. So it was with every experience, with sorrow and joy, with hopes and fears, with doubts and decisions. All were taken by Him into His Father's presence, and there all were discussed and dedicated. For Him, prayer was first, last and all the time, communion with God.

Our prayers can never come alive until we too grasp this inner reality behind them. So often these prayers of ours are no more than a tedious asking for boons or a tortured confession of sins. "Give" and "forgive" are the words most often on our lips when we kneel before God, not "thanks" and "praise" as with Jesus. Indeed, we treat God as though He were an impersonal departmental store, where we bargain for blessings. Yet all the time, He is our Father, loving us with an everlasting love, loving us more than we have ever loved ourselves!

God is no impersonal, *in absentia* deity, but the Father Who is "nearer to us than breathing and closer than hands or feet". He knows us in and out, through and through, and seeks nothing so much as our fellow-ship, our love, our communion. Only on that basis can prayer begin to live in our lives, for only then will we be able to look up and call Him, "Father—Abba", using the intimate lovely language of childhood's faith and love. Only then shall we know, even as also we are known!

> Father-like He tends and spares us;
>   Well our feeble frame He knows;
> In His hands He gently bears us,
>   Rescues us from all our foes:
>   Praise Him!   Praise Him!
>   Praise Him!   Praise Him!
> Widely as His mercy flows.[1]

All this becomes clearer when one turns to a fourth and final feature of our Lord's prayer life, namely, the kind of prayers He offered. His prayers had their own divine dimensions. They reached up to the Throne of Grace, and down to the depths of human infamy and shame, and out across the length and breadth of time and space and eternity. But the most important fact about them for us is that they were so personal and practical and to the point. Jesus never used prayer as an outlet for mere wishful thinking, but prayed about real things, real blessings, real people.

His teaching on prayer makes it clear that He meant us to be practical in our piety. He told His disciples to ask and seek and knock. He taught them to pray for daily bread and forgiveness and guidance. He Himself prayed specifically for groups and indi-viduals, for little children, for those who crucified Him,

[1] Henry Francis Lyte, "Praise, my soul, the King of heaven".

for Simon Peter and Judas Iscariot. The real world of
men and events lived and moved in His prayer life.
Does that hold good of our prayers?

Thank God it does hold good of a multitude of
prayers that rise daily to heaven or otherwise some of
us would be indeed without hope! Would Simon Peter
ever have become an apostle if Christ had not prayed
for him? Would the centurion or the penitent thief
have seen the light if the Saviour had not asked forgiveness for them? Would any of us be where we are
today were it not for the prayers of good men and
women to whom life was prayer and prayer was life,
and who faithfully bore us up into the presence of God?

What a difference it makes to know that we are
being prayed for by someone! I remember the difference it made to my own work in the ministry to
receive a letter many years ago now, from an old lady
whose working days were over but whose ministry of
prayer continued. She wrote from a sunbaked house
in the heart of Africa to say that every Sunday morning at eleven o'clock she prayed for me and my work.
What a difference it made to us as children to see the
closed door of our mother's room, behind which we
knew she was praying for us! What a difference it
makes, as one prepares for the services of the sanctuary, to know that across a thousand leagues of sea
others are bearing us up into the presence of God and
asking that here we may come to worship Him in
spirit and in truth! How poor we would be without
those prayers undergirding us and keeping us strong!
And how much we owe others, how much of grace and
strength we deny others simply because we do not
pray for them as we ought! If only we would make
prayer as large as life, life would become life indeed!

COMMON ATTITUDES TOWARDS CHRIST

XIII

FAITHLESS FAMILIARITY

And Nathaniel said unto him: Can any good thing
come out of Nazareth? Philip saith unto him: Come
and see.

St. John 1:46.

HAD Philip planned to do nothing else but shock and
startle his friend, he could hardly have made a better
calculation than when he told Nathaniel that the
Messiah had come to Nazareth. What he said in effect
was that after these long centuries of waiting, watching
and wondering, now in their own day God had at last
revealed Himself, had sent His own special Messenger
among them, His Messiah, "Jesus of Nazareth, the son
of Joseph". It was an astounding statement, breath-
taking in its significance: but the thing which rendered
it almost completely incredible from Nathaniel's point
of view was that final assertion that Messiah was "a
man of Nazareth".

It was hard enough to believe that prophecy had
at last found its fulfilment, and that after all these
countless generations when men had seen only "through
a glass darkly", now they were to see face to face. That
was difficult enough, but to claim that of all places in
the world Nazareth was the locus of this revelation
seemed to Nathaniel quite preposterous. Nazareth,
the next village to his own native Cana! Why, as a boy
he had wandered a hundred times over those four miles
of hill to explore its crooked little streets and its
crowded bazaar. Nazareth had been the happy hunt-

ing ground of many a youthful adventure, and Nazareth folk were his nearest neighbours!

Yet here was Philip claiming in all seriousness that there he would find the Messiah, the Lord's Anointed One, the longed-for Deliverer of his people, Israel. To Nathaniel it sounded utterly impossible, for his very familiarity with Nazareth bred a complete scepticism within him. He knew this place as he knew the back of his own hand, and it seemed utterly ridiculous that anything wonderful or divine could ever happen there. Familiarity, if it had not bred contempt, had at least bred faithlessness in Nathaniel's heart where Nazareth was concerned. Hence his incredulous response to Philip's declaration: "Can any good thing come out of Nazareth?"

Jesus came out of Nazareth. It was in this unpretentious, uninspiring small country town that He lived. It was here that He went to school and attended the synagogue, and learned His trade and grew to the towering stature of the world's Saviour. So that "out of Nazareth" there came not merely "a good thing" but the greatest and best of all God's gifts to men, Jesus of Nazareth.

"Can any good thing come out of Nazareth?" Nathaniel is by no means the only person who has fallen into the sin of faithlessness through the snare of familiarity. All are guilty here at sometime or another. In all, familiarity has bred contempt and scepticism. Our very nearness to the solemn and sacred things of God has ofttimes blinded us to their true character, and we have walked on the holy ground of some Nazareth only to despise it. Yet it is with the foolish and weak things of the world that God confounds the wise and mighty!

There is, for example, the Christian Church. Born at its very door and brought up within its four walls, we are certainly familiar with it. From the day we could first walk we have attended its schools and classes and services. Sunday by Sunday finds us in our own familiar pew, and week after week we are engaged in its active service. Most of us know our Church as well as we know our own homes, and few things in life are more familiar.

If, however, someone were to make the assertion that within this Church we would come face to face with the Living God; that here we would confront the greatest crisis of life, a crisis which would not only change our entire outlook upon the world, but alter the whole course of the future, what response would we make to such a claim? I think I can tell you. With our hearts if not with our voices, we would echo Nathaniel: "Can any good thing come out of our Church?" "Don't talk nonsense!" we would say. "Nothing like that ever happens in our Church. I know, for I have lived and worked in it for years. You certainly cannot tell me anything about my Church that I do not know, and I do know that that is not the kind of religion encountered there. Can any good thing come out of Nazareth?"

This familiarity, which breeds such contempt for the Church and such faithlessness in God's omnipotent power to save and redeem our lives, is one of the greatest perils confronting Christian people. It has been said that "we can be so inoculated by small doses of Christianity that we can't catch the big thing" and that has happened to many. Indeed, for multitudes to-day the real tragedy is simply that they do not believe there is anything more to be found in religion than

what they themselves have found in it, which is next to
nothing.   Church services have become a drug; the
reading of the Scriptures a soporific; the singing of the
psalms and hymns a mere emotional ecstasy.   Familiarity blocks us out from the dynamic experiences of
the saints, and conventional Christian upbringing has
become like a millstone about our necks.

These are hard words but true.   Yet the most
devastating utterances that ever came from our Lord's
lips were spoken, not to the non-church goer, but to
the most scrupulous and regular church attenders of
His day, the Scribes and Pharisees.   It was they whom
He called "a generation of vipers", "whited sepul-
chres", "hypocrites", and against them He directed all
the withering fire of His consuming wrath.   And was
the sin of the Scribes and Pharisees not simply that
they believed there could be nothing more in religion
than what they themselves had found there?   Familiarity had blinded them to the infinite possibilities of
God's love and power.   To those same infinite possibilities, familiarity still blinds men.

The real truth of course is that to attend church is
about the most dangerous thing anyone of us can
possibly do.   For this is God's Church and He is here.
This is Christ's body and He is in the midst.   At any
moment the Sword of His Spirit may descend upon us
to pierce the armour of our pride and self-righteousness
and sin and leave us naked and defenceless.   At any
hour His voice may sound in our hearts and electrify
us into action, sending us forth to challenge the world
and do battle with the principalities and powers which
seek to rule it.   "Can any good thing come out of this
Nazareth?"   Without question it can.   For Christ is in
His Church and what we despise God delights in; what

we discard God uses. In His Providence this simple
place, this unadorned service, may well become pregnant with everlasting destiny and eternal significance
for all who worship here.

Again the peril of familiarity is frequently seen in
the attitude which we adopt towards ourselves. The
one place where most men reveal a commendable humility is in discussing the quality and character of
their own Christian discipleship. Most of us imagine
that we can do at least one job of work with a fair
degree of skill, while a few would have themselves
masters of every trade. But turn to the question of
where we stand with God, and how we are following in
the footsteps of our Lord and Saviour Jesus Christ,
and how different is our attitude! Here all self-
confidence forsakes us, and we refuse to make anything
but the most meagre claims. "I know I'm not perfect" is the refrain that one hears with dull monotony.
We are what we are, and that is the end of it. We
certainly are not saints, nor are we aspirants after
sainthood.

But why so sudden a change from self-confidence
to self-deprecation? Is the answer not that familiarity
with self has bred contempt? We know only too well
our own failings and foibles, our sins and selfishnesses,
and we have come to accept them as inevitable and
inescapable handicaps. We feel ourselves in the grip
of an inscrutable fate which finds expression in the
unhappy confession, "I am as I am and nothing can
change me." The last of our thoughts is that humble,
stumbling, sinful "I" could by the grace of God be
reformed and transformed into a radiant, triumphant
Christian disciple with power to overcome every sin

and selfishness. Instead we acquiesce in our sins, submit to our weaknesses, and allow every noble aspiration to be crushed out of existence by the tyranny of old evil habits.

Every visitor to a portrait gallery knows how impossible it is to see the whole picture by standing close to the canvas. To understand and appreciate the artist's work, one must stand well back, so that the eye can see it as a whole and not simply in small sections. So it is when we look at our own lives and characters. We must stand back from the canvas and see them as a whole. In other words, it is never enough to see in ourselves only what we have been and what we are. We must also see what we ought to be and what by the grace of God we can become.

In any reckoning of our lives then, God must be taken into account. Without God, no good thing could ever have come out of Nazareth. Nor can you and I ever hope to be other than we are in our own strength. Yet with God, Nazareth sent forth Jesus Christ; Nazareth became a corner of heaven, a gateway to glory, a door leading to a new heaven and a new earth. And the same can happen within the Nazareth of our own lives; for with God we too can become more than conquerors.

In this mortal conflict not one of us stands alone, God is with us. In Him we live and move and have our being; and behind the puny strength of will and purpose are the infinite resources of His immortal strength. Through Him, you and I—ordinary mortals that we are—can be changed into very extraordinary Christian disciples, radiant and victorious followers of Jesus of Nazareth. For with God these defeated,

despairing, disappointed lives of ours can send forth
such Christlike character, such triumphant faith, such
abounding hope that nothing will ever again be
impossible to us. "All things will be ours, for we are
Christ's and Christ is God's."

> Fight the good fight
> With all thy might;
> Christ is thy strength, and Christ thy right;
> Lay hold on life, and it shall be
> Thy joy and crown eternally.[1]

Yet the most serious of all the sins of familiarity
is to adopt Nathaniel's attitude of scepticism and
unbelief towards Christ Himself, so that once again
familiarity breeds faithlessness.

There is no figure in human history better known
than that of Jesus of Nazareth. From the day we
could first talk, His name has been upon our lips; His
image before our eyes; His words in our hearts.
Through all these long years we have been hearing
about Him, learning about Him, talking about Him.
To Him we have learned to pray, and in Him have
been taught to believe. The truth is that Jesus of
Nazareth is as familiar to most of us as our own
shadow; but the tragedy is that for many of us He is
no more real to us than our shadow.

We know all of the background of His life. We
know Nazareth as though it were our own home town.
But have we come to know the central figure Himself,
Jesus the Christ, the Saviour of the World? To know
about Him is the poorest possible substitute for know-

[1] J. S. B. Monsell, "Fight the good fight".

ing Him. And what shall it profit anyone of us if, knowing all the facts of His life and death and resurrection, we yet miss the Faith which can roll away twenty centuries and bring Him, a Living Saviour, to our side and into our hearts today? No wonder there are defeated lives tyrannized over by sin. If Jesus Christ means no more to the world than this, then was it worth His while going to Calvary and dying upon its Cross?

"Can any good thing come out of Nazareth?" Can Jesus possibly step out of that picture in which memory and imagination have framed Him and become a living, mighty power in our lives today? Can we know Him as the disciples knew Him, as Master, and Saviour and ever-loving Friend? That is the incredible miracle which the Gospels proclaim. Jesus of Nazareth does come out of the picture and meet us face to face, as living soul with living soul; and because this is possible, our lives can even now begin their most thrilling chapter of adventure and achievement, of joy and triumph in the strength and by the side of this wonderful Saviour.

But how can this miracle take place, and the blindness of familiarity give place to that vision where we shall see our Lord face to face? The only satisfactory answer is that with which Philip met Nathaniel's scepticism. Philip did not argue with his friend, for no argument could ever have proved the truth of his claim. Nor can any argument ever prove to us that Christ is alive and that He can change weakness into strength and sinfulness into saintliness. More than argument is needed. Hence Philip's invitation to

Nathaniel: "Come and see. Come and prove by your own experience that Christ is alive and in our midst." And Nathaniel went and saw; he tried and tested, and in the end was convinced and converted.

There is no other way than this to the living Lord. "Come and see." Shake yourself loose from the paralysing philosophy of familiarity which claims that there is nothing more to be known about Christ than what we already know; that there is nothing better in store than what we have already found; and that Jesus of Nazareth is no more real than any other man can be after two thousand years have rolled past. Have done with that imprisoning creed, and for once make a great venture of faith. "Come and see." Put the New Testament message to the test. Put the Living Christ to the test. "Believe on the Lord Jesus Christ", not as someone who was alive and is dead; not merely as an example nor as an ideal. But believe in Him as a Living Person, Who walks this way of life with us; Who speaks in all goodness and beauty and truth and love; and Who is able and ready to do for us more than we can ever ask or think.

"Believe in Him" and you shall be saved! "Come and see" and you shall find One whose Name is "Wonderful, Counsellor, The Mighty God, the Everlasting Father, the Prince of Peace". Most wonderful of all, you will discover, as Nathaniel did, that this Living and Everlasting Lord knows about you, has been watching you, and waiting for you, and is ready to welcome you. I tell you there is no discovery in the world like this discovery; no joy so wonderful; no fellowship so blessed; no peace so surpassing. "Come and see."

XIV

PERSONAL PREJUDICE

And they did not receive Him, because His face was
as though He would go to Jerusalem.

St. Luke 9:53.

It was at the close of a long, exhausting day that
Jesus and His disciples met with this chilling inhos-
pitality at the hands of those Samaritan villagers.
That morning, before the sun had risen above the hills
of Moab, the Master and His men had started from
Nazareth, skirting first the shoulder of Mount Tabor
and then dropping down into the broad plain of Esdraelon. Under a burning sun, they had crossed the
plain to push, late in the afternoon, into the gashed,
torn highlands of Samaria. And now, with the sun
setting behind Carmel, with limbs aching, and with
feet powdered by the dust of many miles, they called
a halt before this Samaritan village in the hope of
finding here a night's lodging.

Yet the only welcome awaiting them was a rough
hostile refusal. No one would give them lodging! No
one would welcome them to a seat at the fire and a
share in the evening meal. Instead doors were slammed
on their faces; gates were barred; and everywhere a
bad-tempered hostility evinced. The whole reception
or lack of it was almost incredible, particularly among
an eastern people famed for their hospitality and
courtesy towards strangers.

What explanation have we got for this shocking
ungraciousness? Luke suggests a reason. It was, he

says, because our Lord's face "was as though He would
go to Jerusalem", or, to quote Dr. Weymouth's trans-
lation, "Because He was evidently going to Jerusalem",
an explanation both original and significant.

The first thought which suggests itself on hearing
this reason is that it was manifestly insincere. Could
anyone possibly refuse Christ hospitality just because
He was going to Jerusalem? I am afraid that with
many Samaritans, and with men of other races also, it
was not only possible but highly probable. A large
proportion of the inhabitants of Samaria would have
refused Christ the hospitality of their homes simply
because He was a Jew going to worship at Jerusalem,
and not a Samaritan bound for Mount Gerizim.

The antipathy was, of course, mutual. The Jews
would have no dealings with the Samaritans, and they
in turn responded by heartily hating the Jews. Conse-
quently when it was clear that our Lord was bound for
Jerusalem, all the old hatreds and animosities stirred
within their breasts and they slammed their doors in
His face. Perhaps had He been bound in the opposite
direction, they might have been persuaded to offer Him
hospitality, but nothing would make them entertain
One who could have any dealings with their natural
enemies. Jesus was rejected because He would have
no part in their national prejudices.

This was, of course, by no means the only occasion
when our Lord found Himself rejected because of
racial prejudices. Read the Gospels and the Acts and
it becomes very clear that one of the major factors
which brought Him to Golgotha was racial prejudice.
If the Samaritans rejected Him because His face was
set towards Jerusalem, the Jews rejected Him because

He was not only prepared to accept but also to give hospitality to all kinds and conditions of men, to publicans and sinners, to Gentiles as well as Jews, to Samaritans and Greeks and Romans. They crucified Him because His sympathies were too broad, His views were too advanced, His love was too free and unprejudiced and boundless. This Teacher and Prophet who consorted with men and women of all races and classes was too dangerous a person to have at large. Much better get Him out of the way, and make sure that the key would remain turned in the door of their narrow bigotry and their cruel prejudices!

Turning to the Acts, we find that it was on this very issue that the young Christian Church had to face the greatest crisis of its early years. The Church had not long been established, when the question arose as to whether or not the Gentiles were to be admitted into its communion. James, who was the leader of the pro-Jewish section within the Church, was all for keeping out non-Jews. Simon Peter, after his vision at Joppa and the call which followed it from the Roman Centurion, was at first inclined to a liberal view, but afterwards recanted and joined the strict Jewish party. It was left therefore to St. Paul to do battle against this monstrous evil, and he did so with typical fearlessness. Read the account of the conflict as he has given it in the Epistle to the Galatians. He alone withstood the apostles. For him "there was neither Jew nor Greek, bond nor free, male nor female". "All were one in Christ",[1] and Paul knew no rest until the doors were flung wide open so that all the world might come to Christ.

Yet if our Lord and His greatest apostle had no

[1] Galatians 3:28.

part in racial prejudices, the same cannot be said of all
His followers.   You will remember W. N. Ewer's
quatrain:

> How odd
> Of God
> To choose
> The Jews.[1]

To which Cecil Browne replied so pointedly:

> But not so odd
> As those who choose
> A Jewish God
> Yet spurn the Jews.[2]

Hand in hand with Christianity down the centuries has
gone the evil spirit of racial prejudice and class hatreds,
and to this day too many people remain who would
rather give up their Christianity than surrender their
hatred of Jews, or Negroes, of Germans, or Japanese
or French.   Mahatma Gandhi being turned out of a
Christian Church in Cape Town, or a Negro being
lynched in the United States or the Jews or Japanese
being persecuted in Ottawa or Vancouver, these things
are all too common among those who profess Christ as
Lord.

Yet can we remain Christians and continue to
harbour such hatreds?   Have we not in fact already
abandoned Christ and Christianity when we give
hospitality to such bitter, blind prejudices?   It seems
to me that if this incident from the Gospel means anything at all, it means that there can be no room for
Christ in the heart that has room for racial animosities

---

[1] W. N. Ewer, in *Weekend Book, Vol. I,* ed. Francis and Vera
Meynell. The Dial Press.

[2] Cecil Browne, in *Weekend Book Vol. I.*

and class hatreds. "He that loveth not, knoweth not God," declares John, "for God is love."[1] "He that loveth not his brother abideth in death. Whosoever hateth his brother is a murderer, and no murderer hath eternal life."[2] Fill your soul with these things, harbour hatred, nurse prejudice, give house room to any antipathies against your brother man, and there is no room for Christ. Keep such company within the soul, and we must part company with its Saviour!

But look again at this reason for rejecting Christ. Ostensibly the Samaritans rejected our Lord because He was a Jew and not a man of their own race; and though this was no doubt true of the majority, one suspects that not a few used racial prejudice simply as a cover and excuse behind which to hide a personal sloth. Some at least among them were too tired, too lazy, too self-engrossed to be put to the trouble entailed in preparing beds and providing a meal for this Stranger and His friends. They could not and would not be bothered. So Jesus and His men were turned back into the night and must needs seek shelter elsewhere.

This reason too, still holds good, and there are many, too many, who reject Christ simply because they have no desire to be disturbed by Him. His coming into life would certainly mean a disturbance, for some a revolution, and we have little liking for disturbances, and no desire at all for revolutions. Indeed the one thing most of us are determined upon is to maintain the status quo, the even tenor of our ways!

The result is that we cling to orthodoxy in our beliefs and maintain our connection with the official

[1] 1 John 4:8.
[2] 1 John 3:14, 15.

Church; but the personal, living Christ, the unpredictable Christ, is carefully locked out from the inner sanctuary of our lives. We like our religion but we like it to be carefully docketed and easily put away like a will or an insurance policy. Heaven forbid that the living, vital, all-commanding Lord should ever burst in upon us and take the citadel of our souls by storm! That would be far too catastrophic, far too revolutionary, far too dangerous for peace and happiness! So Jesus is kept carefully outside. Like the Samaritans of old, we slam our doors upon His Face when He appears, and tumble back into our narrow little beds of self-centred ease and comfort.

There is no doubt at all that we have here one of the greatest hindrances and handicaps confronting the Christian Church. Into its communion come so many who want religion on their own terms, not on God's terms. They will subscribe to its creeds, provided we do not take them too seriously. They will contribute a little but not too much to its treasury. They will give a tardy attendance at its services and sacraments. But all the time, religion is on their terms, not on God's. Like those Samaritans, they demand their own particular Mount Gerizim; their own specially expurgated version of the Scriptures, their own peculiar rites and privileges. But challenge them with a little more devotion, with a little more prayerfulness, with a little more real self-sacrifice and service and the doors are shut and bolted; the blinds are drawn; and nothing on earth will stir them from the fastnesses of their slumbers!

The fact is that there are some who do not want the Living Christ. Give Him to us embalmed in two thousand years of history and we shall accept Him.

Offer Him to us in the gorgeous sarcophagus of ancient creed and confession, and we shall burn the incense of worship before Him. But God forbid that He should come alive. We want no Living Lord thundering at the door of our hearts, asking to be taken in and given the hospitality of our lives. Such a Christ we fear. From such a Christ we flee, for if Jesus of Nazareth were to come alive within our lives, what revolutions He would compel us to make! What transformations would have to take place!

O you foolish Samaritans, how can you be so blind? You poor benighted souls, suffocating to death in that miserable hovel you have built in place of the glorious palace God planned for you in the beginning! Of course this religion of yours is a fake and a falsehood, as any religion that is man-made must be! And some day you will probably find it out, but then it may be too late to make amends. For then life will be wasted and the day of opportunity past, and the hour of judgment at hand. And a dying man can seldom creep from his bed even to unlatch the door for Christ.

The other day a lad of fourteen in all seriousness told his father that he was an atheist, and when pressed for his reasons replied that religion was simply a waste of time. "I don't know this God they talk about. He means nothing to me. Why should I waste time attending chapel and reading the Bible when I might be doing much more interesting things?" That lad had an honesty that some of us sadly lack. He knew that a God who is not a living God is no god at all; and that religion which is simply embalmed history is of a great deal less value than a thousand other things in life.

Of course, the only God worthy of man's devotion and the only God capable of man's salvation is the Living God, the Living Christ Who marches triumphantly into our lives to disturb them to the innermost recesses of our being. That Lord alone can save our souls and set us free from bondage to fears and hatreds and miserable prejudices and blinding passions; and throw open wide the doors and windows of life so that all the pure, clean winds of God can blow in upon us to cleanse and renew our souls. Yet some of us have been keeping Him out!

"Behold, I stand at the door and knock",[1] and He is there knocking now, this living, triumphant Lord. And we can hear Him knocking—knocking in conscience, in ideals, in all the loveliness of love and truth and beauty. But will we answer His knock? Will we open the door, and give Him our lives? So often before we have turned Him away. But perhaps now you will open the door and invite Him in to sup with you, and you with Him?

> Batter my heart, three person'd God; for, you
> As yet but knock, breathe, shine and seek to mend.
>
> Take me to you, imprison me, for I
> Except you enthrall me, never shall be free,
> Nor ever chaste, except you ravish me.[2]

[1] Revelation 3:20.
[2] John Donne, *Holy Sonnets*, xiv.

XV

CORRUPT CURIOSITY

Now when Herod saw Jesus, he was exceeding glad;
for he was of a long time desirous to see him, because
he had heard concerning him; and he hoped to see
some miracle done by him. And he questioned him
in many words; but he answered him nothing.

St. Luke 23:8-9 (R.V.)

WHO, we may well ask, was this man who was "greatly
delighted to see Jesus", who had "long wanted to see
Him", and who "hoped to see Him perform some
miracle"? What manner of person was he who "put
many questions" to our Lord, and was answered in the
most significant and eloquent of all ways—by silence?
The answer is Herod Antipas, a man who played a not
insignificant part in the events recorded in the New
Testament. It will be well to recall some of the high-
lights of his life in order that we may understand the
background to this particular incident recorded by St.
Luke.

Herod Antipas was the fifth son of Herod the
Great, that evil genius whose name will be for ever
associated with the massacre of the Innocents at
Bethlehem and who died soon after the birth of our
Lord. Under his will, his son Antipas received Perea
and Galilee as his portion with the title of Tetrarch.
When Pilate therefore heard that Jesus was a Galilean,
he immediately sent Him to Herod in the hope of thus

finding an easy escape out of the dilemma in which he found himself.

In the New Testament, Herod Antipas is remembered largely by three things. In the first place, he is known as the wrecker both of his own and his brother's home. While visiting Rome as the guest of his brother Philip, Herod persuaded his sister-in-law, Herodias, to leave her husband and return with him to Palestine, and this despite the fact that he was already married to the daughter of the King of Arabia. On their arrival in Palestine, his legal wife left him and returned to her father's palace. The result was war in which Herod's forces were severely beaten by the armies of Arabia.

Licentiousness and lust, however, were but the first steps in his degradation. They led, as they so often still do, to a complete disregard of all justice, so that Herod first had John the Baptist imprisoned and then, to fulfil a crazed drunken vow made to Salome, Herodias' daughter, had him finally beheaded. John, you recall, had incurred Herod's hatred by his utterly fearless denunciation of the king's private life, and for long months he pined in one of the dark dungeons of the gloomy fortress of Machaerus overlooking the Dead Sea. It was during this period that Jesus sent him a message of hope and encouragement, a message not so much of words as of deeds, of actions rather than arguments, so that the Baptist's faith was revived and new grace given him to endure the bondage of imprisonment. But the sand was fast running through the glass of his life, and one night when the palace above echoed and re-echoed to the wild revellings of the king, the bolt was shot back in the prison door, and John, old before his years, was led forth to lay his head upon the executioner's block. His warfare was accomplished, and Herod had added murder to his many crimes.

Finally this man is remembered by reason of the part he played in the trial of our Lord. Jesus had grown up and spent most of his public ministry within the territory of Antipas. At first on hearing of this new prophet, the king had shown a superstitious interest, imagining in his guilt that this was John the Baptist restored to life again.[1] Later he sought to lay hands upon the Master, and a group of friendly Pharisees advised that He should flee the country. You remember Christ's answer. More clearly than anything it reveals the contempt in which our Lord held this puppet king. "Go," he said, "and tell that fox, Behold, I cast out devils, and I do cures today and tomorrow, and the third day I shall be perfected . . . It cannot be that a prophet perish out of Jerusalem."[2]

So it was that not until Jesus had come for the last time "to be perfected" at Jerusalem did Herod see Him face to face. Then we read "he was greatly delighted". A long cherished desire seemed about to be fulfilled for one not accustomed to wait for the fulfilment of any of his whims. Herod saw Christ. At great length he questioned Him. But Herod neither saw a miracle, nor did he hear one word from the lips of the Saviour of the World. The king of Galilee was received by the King of Kings with an absolute and unbroken silence!

In describing Herod's attitude towards our Lord as "corrupt curiosity", no one can question the justice of that description; nor can there be any doubt that here we have portrayed for us perhaps the most hopeless,

[1] Matthew 14:2.
[2] Luke 13: 32-33.

the most spiritually barren and morally destructive attitude which any human being can adopt towards Jesus of Nazareth.

There is a curiosity which is positive and valuable, for it is inspired by a deep craving for truth and a sincere desire to discover a real and living way across the trackless wastes of time. The Greeks, for example, when they came to Jesus were impelled by this positive, constructive type of curiosity, while both the Gospels and the Acts contain many other instances of a curiosity which led to conviction and finally to consecration. Curiosity, the right kind of curiosity, can be a very lode star guiding our feet to the cradle of the King.

But there is another type of curiosity, a curiosity which contains within itself its own terrible doom, and of this type Herod is the sorry representative. He had "long wanted to see" Jesus, not because he was interested in either His Person or His Message, but simply because he wanted to be amused. Long years ago this man had got beyond any vital interest in his own moral or spiritual wellbeing. Indeed, all that mattered to him now was to kill time, to drive off boredom, to flog into activity his failing appetites and flagging interests. So Jesus of Nazareth was received with the same expectancy by Herod as he would have received an Indian snake-charmer or a Roman jester. And to this man Christ had not one word to say!

There can surely be no more damning attitude towards Christ and Christianity than this attitude of idle, corrupt curiosity, and yet such an attitude is by no means unknown. Indeed, it is not necessary to commit Herod's crimes in order to adopt Herod's attitude towards Christ.   All that is necessary is that we adopt towards ourselves what was his attitude towards himself.   For corrupt curiosity is the direct product of a complete and utter self-centredness.   Herod lived for one thing and one thing only, his own self-gratification, and that led him to disregard the sanctity of marriage, to despise the laws of justice and righteousness, and defy the sacredness of human life.   Let a man live only for his own self-gratification and there is no crime of which he will not be capable, no evil to which he will not give hospitality, no sacrilege he will not commit, not even that of mocking God and making of His Son a jeer and a jest.

The desperate thing, of course, is that in every one of us are to be found the seeds of this evil thing.   All our lives we have to do battle against its rank growth, if our souls are not to be choked and destroyed by it. We must constantly be examining ourselves.   We must keep "crucifying the flesh with the affections and lusts thereof".[1] We must "keep under our bodies" and prune mercilessly our selfish desires and ambitions.   Above all things we must "live in the Spirit and walk in the Spirit", for only those who "sow to the Spirit shall of the Spirit reap life everlasting."[2]

Life for every one of us is a battle, a battle between the evil cancerous growth of self-centred gratification, and the clean healthy growth of God-centred selfless-ness.   No truer word ever came from the lips of Jesus than His declaration that "whosoever will save his life shall lose it; and whosoever will lose his life for My sake

[1] Galatians 5:24.
[2] Galatians 6:8.

shall find it."[1]   How then does the battle go within
our souls?   Is the day with God, or have we given the
victory, as Herod did, to self?

Two great and glorious opportunities opened before
Herod that day when Christ stood before Him, opportunities which, alas! he rejected for ever.

In the first place, Herod had the opportunity of
discovering for himself the true and living way of life
and forsaking the downward way of death upon which
he had so long travelled.   This man's soul had never
known a greater moment.   In that hour the sinner
could have repented of his sin; the sensualist could
have turned from the bondage of his flesh; the moral
coward could have broken the bands of his fear; and
turned to the long arduous ascent which led through
repentance to reparation and righteousness. But Herod
did none of these things.   Indeed, there is not the
slightest indication that he had the desire to do any of
them.   For the man was morally and spiritually dead,
and nothing that God could do for him, nothing that
Christ might say, could penetrate to the grim depths
into which he had doomed his own soul.

It is a dread, awful thought that each one of us has
within ourselves the power to put ourselves beyond
the reach of God's mercy and forgiving, saving love.
We, and not God, can cast ourselves into hell.   We can
banish ourselves forever from His face.   We can doom
and damn the precious life that is ours.

Yet God is so infinite in His mercy and love that to
the very last He stands before us and gives to each one
the opportunity of forsaking the way of death and
choosing the way of life.   Even Herod the murderer is

[1] Matthew 16:25.

given a last chance. Even the dying thief is confronted
by the Lord. God in Christ will not leave us alone but
is forever standing and pleading with us to turn from
our sin and follow Him.

> To-day the Saviour calls:
>   Ye wanderers, come;
> O ye benighted souls,
>   Why longer roam?
>
> To-day the Saviour calls:
>   For refuge fly;
> The storm of justice falls,
>   And death is nigh.[1]

"Come then and let us return unto the Lord, for He
will have mercy upon us; and to our God for He will
abundantly pardon."[2]

Finally, Herod that day had the great opportunity
of setting at liberty Jesus of Nazareth, the Saviour of
the World. Pilate had sent the Lord to him because as
a man of Nazareth He came under Herod's jurisdic-
tion. But Herod turned judgment into jesting, and
made justice a mockery. Jesus, who might have walked
out of his presence free, went forth bound and in
chains, went forth to His death upon the Cross.

How, I wonder, does Jesus of Nazareth walk out of
our presence? We can send Him forth bound as Herod
did, as Pilate did. We can hamper and hinder Him so
that His life is obstructed and His kingdom blocked
and barred. We can refuse Him His liberty. We can
stop His lips and silence the beating of His heart and
banish Him to His grave. But to do that is not to

[1] S. F. Smith.

[2] Isaiah 55:7.

destroy Christ but to destroy ourselves. It is our lives that are bound, our lips that are stopped, our doom that is sealed, our destruction that is assured.

On the other hand, praise be to God, we have it still within our power to give the Lord His liberty. We can cut away the thongs which bind Him and strike off the chains which hold Him. We can give Him His freedom and cast ourselves utterly upon His mercy, so that in us and through us He may go forth to do His mighty saving, redeeming work in this world. Give Christ His freedom, freedom within your conscience and will, within your heart and mind, freedom among all your possessions and privileges, freedom to do with you what He will, and you too will make the discovery that "the best is yet to be, the last of life for which the first was made."[1] You will find with Augustine and Bunyan and Wesley and Schweitzer and Grenfell, yes, with the saints of all ages that life begins again, life richer, fuller, more abundant than you had ever believed possible. For then you will have learned that life's greatest secret is not to possess the freedom which can do as it desires, but to be so possessed by the love of God and of His Christ, that by losing ourselves to Him we are rich and free. Only then can our restless souls find their true rest in Him; for we are "bound until He lays His strong hand upon us, in bondage until we become His slaves, dead until we give up our lives to Him". Give Christ His freedom! Let Him live in you that you may truly live in Him!

[1] Robert Browning, "Rabbi ben Ezra".

XVI

SUBLIME SUBSERVIENCE

Then cometh Jesus . . . unto John to be baptized of
him. But John forbad him saying, I have need to be
baptized of thee, and comest thou to me?

ST. MATTHEW 3:13-14.

"THE HISTORY of the world," wrote Carlyle, "is but the
biography of great men", which reminds one of the
remark of President Harrison at a Memorial Address
to his former commander, General Grant. "Great lives,"
he said, "never go out. They go on." It is just such a
life that is conjured up before us by these ancient words
of Scripture, a life that despite the ever-rolling stream
of time still goes on.

Of all the persons surrounding the earthly ministry
of Jesus of Nazareth, there was none cast in a larger
mould, none who attained to more towering splendours
of character than John the Baptist. This man stood
out as a giant among pygmies. It was no ordinary man,
for example, who could draw such a constant crowd of
pilgrims from every corner of the land, out into the
wildnesses of the Judean wilderness. Men came to him
from every quarter, out of every class, and submitted
with unbelievable humility both to his judgments and
ordinances. His preaching, too, revealed his pre-
eminence. His was a direct, soul-searching, challeng-
ing Gospel. John toyed with no mere pleasantries,
suffered no illusions, judged ruthlessly every hypocrisy.

Read again that sermon which he addressed to the
Pharisees and Sadducees. The man's utter fearlessness,

151

his swift sure diagnosis of their spiritual condition, his rapier-like judgments all witness to his greatness. Not in many generations had the Jewish people come face to face with such a fearless and fearful prophet of righteousness. Indeed, what tribute could have been higher than Christ's own words concerning him: "Among them that are born of women, there hath not arisen a greater than John the Baptist"?

See this man, however, when Jesus first appears before him, and mark the change! All his self-confidence, his cool assurance, his bold ruthless way of dealing with men vanishes, and we are confronted by someone childlike in his humility and self-deprecation. When his cousin makes the request that He might be baptized, John is dumbfounded. He, whose sandal straps he had always considered himself unworthy to fasten, wanted him to do this thing, wanted to be taken down into the waters of his baptism! John could never do that. "Master," we hear him pleading, "I cannot do this thing. I am not worthy. I am no more than just a weak, stumbling sinner myself, while my baptism is nothing compared to that baptism which you can bring to men. This rite that I practise is simply a poor, earthly symbol reserved for miserable sinners, and certainly was never intended for 'the Lamb of God who taketh away the sin of the world'. No, I cannot do this thing that you ask. I have need to be baptized of Thee, and comest thou to me?"

Two things of the very greatest import, two things that are always present when the human and the divine confront each other are brought together in this incident. On the one hand, there is here man's sense of need, his need of God, God's bounty and blessing and baptism. On the other hand, there is here God's

demand for man's help, God's need of man's co-
operation and consecration and companionship. Let
us look at those two conflicting needs and try to discover how under God they can be finally resolved.

Take first of all this deep sense of inadequacy and
need which men have always felt when they have found
themselves confronted by God, and which they have
felt supremely as they have stood face to face with
Jesus Christ. Is there anyone born of woman who
does not share this need with John? Is there anyone
who somewhere along life's pilgrimage does not cry out
for God's help? Voltaire was surely right when he
declared that "If God did not exist, it would be necessary to invent Him."

"What shall I render unto the Lord for all his
benefits toward me?" asks the Psalmist, and his only
answer is to make confession of his need. "I will take
the cup of salvation and call upon the name of the
Lord." What can we possibly offer to God, we who
are creatures of such petty ways? What can we ever
do for Him with our sin-stained hands, and hardened
hearts, and clay-bound feet? Our best moments, when
we are there on our knees before God, find us most
deeply conscious of our worthlessness, pouring out the
confession of a deep, desperate need.

"I have need." It is the perennial cry of all living
religion. You can hear it like the sough of the wind or
the sigh of the sea across all continents and among all
peoples. "Thou hast made us for Thyself and our
hearts are restless until they find their rest in Thee."
"To be a Seeker," said Cromwell, "is to be of the best
sect next to the finders", and we are all Seekers. For
the heart knows what sometimes the reason does not

know that man cannot save himself. Only the grace of God working in and through him can do that, and real life is not so much a matter of finding oneself as being found of God; not a question of possessing something, but of being possessed by Someone. "I live", yes, but that is nothing, cries St. Paul, it is "Christ that lives in me" which gives my life its real worth.

No wonder, then, that the greatest hymns of Christendom are simply one passionate cry of need, man's endless, insatiable need of God. We can all sing with Toplady,

> Nothing in my hand I bring,
> Simply to Thy Cross I cling;

or with Wesley,

> Other refuge have I none;
> Hangs my helpless soul on Thee.

or again with St. Bernard,

> Our restless spirits yearn for Thee,
> Where'er our changeful lot is cast.

"I have need!" Of course we have, every one of us, the best with the worst, the Johns with the Judases, the saints with the sinners. Let no one be ashamed to confess that need. In the things of the spirit, it is those who have no need to confess who are the shameless ones.

It is, of course, in the presence of Christ that we realize the full depth of our need. John, as he confronted the Pharisees in their livery of stiff self-righteousness, had little consciousness of his personal need. All he knew or thought of then was that these self-appointed leaders of religion were lagging desperately behind, and his anger blazed out against them like withering flame. But the moment Christ stood before him, the whole poverty of his own life and stuntedness of his own soul were suddenly laid bare.

It is in the presence of Christ that the best with the worst find their true level. No one can strut or preen himself there. Self-righteousness falls from us like worn out rags, and with bowed heads and hearts we confess our need and cry out for mercy and compassion. "If Shakespeare were to come into this room, we should all rise to our feet," Charles Lamb remarked one evening to a group of friends, "but if Jesus Christ were to come in, then we would all get down on our knees." You cannot do anything but kneel there, kneel as a suppliant.

> Just as I am, poor, wretched, blind,—
> Sight, riches, healing of the mind,
> Yea, all I need, in Thee to find,
>   O Lamb of God, I come.

Turn now to the other aspect of this meeting between the Divine and the Human. It is not only man who cries, "I have need", but God also. That is the incredible message behind this incident. God confronts us for the purpose of using us. He claims our service; demands our co-operation; expects our companionship.

Here is the most stupendous thing which can happen to any man or woman, and yet it is something which is constantly recurring in life. God in Jesus Christ confronts John and insists upon receiving his baptism. He meets young, tongue-tied Jeremiah, and demands that he go forth and speak to a nation in His Name. Out into the wilderness He follows Elijah, hunts him down in his secret lair, and tells him that it is his still small voice that He wants to be heard above the raging of the world's tempest and the rumblings of its earthquake.

Other instances crowd to mind. You may be a tinker lying in a Bedford Jail with nothing but a pen in your hand, and a dream in your heart, but God will have them. You may be a brilliant Don, sharpening your wits against all the philosophies of the world and dallying with its pleasures, as young Augustine did at Hippo, but when God claims your mind and heart and soul, there can be no denying Him. Or you may be a young doctor attached to a great London Hospital with dreams of Harley Street colouring the future, yet if God wants you He will take you some night into a religious meeting, as he did with Wilfred Grenfell of Labrador; or perhaps just put a magazine on your desk some morning, as he did with Dr. Schweitzer of the Congo: and again you will rise up and answer His call.

God has need of us, and those things in life, those gifts, talents, abilities, powers which we ourselves rate so low, which in fact we may regard more as handicaps than gifts, He asks for and claims for His service. The Divine need overrules the human need, and men who are weak, ignorant, foolish, poor, again and again find themselves pressed into a service for which they feel sure they have no real gifts and less grace.

There is a strange ruthlessness about the way in which He deals with us here, a ruthlessness which shows itself in two ways.

In the first place, though our needs may be mountainous God brushes them aside. He refuses to look at the long debit account which we present to

Him. What interests Him, and what He insists upon our using in His service is the pitifully small credit balance which remains over. He wants John's simple baptism of water, Peter's unpolished frankness, Matthew's penmanship and gift of detail, Paul's school-room learning. God wants the thing we have got to give Him, not what we would like to be able to give Him.

Remember that the next time He knocks at your door, and claims your support. It is only what we have got to give that He wants, that and nothing more. Nor does it matter to Him what we may think of our offering. What does matter is that He can and will use the gift if we but give it.

Then again, the ruthlessness of God's dealings with us is seen in this further fact that so often He asks from us the very thing we were constrained to ask from Him. John, for example, wanted the baptism of fire from on high, but his Lord wanted his own simple baptism of Jordan's water. Or the multitudes cried out for bread, but Christ's response was to ask, "How many loaves have ye?" The sick pleaded for health, the sinners for power; but each time His answer was to have faith, to claim health and power as a right and live in all the abounding riches of those who are the sons of God. So often God asks the very thing we ask from Him!

There is divine wisdom in all this, for it is by attempting the impossible that we attain to the impossible. Every mother knows this, when she holds out open arms and insists upon her child taking his first step alone. And God in heaven, who watches over us with more than a mother's love and care knows that we must use the gift He has given us, or it will atrophy and perish. We must circulate, not bury, life's precious talents. We must answer His call and give, however small the gift.

I remember as a student sharing a month with the late John McNeill, whose name as an evangelist will live on. For an hour and more he could hold great audiences spell-bound, as few others could do, driving home to the hearts and consciences of his hearers the mighty lessons of the Gospel. Yet the man who preached with such power was utterly different from the person who waited in the vestry before the service began. "Pray for me," he would plead, "Pray for me!" It was a child who shivered there on the brink of a tremendous undertaking. His gift seemed so small, so inadequate, so paltry compared to the great task to which he was called. Yet he gave it and God used it beyond all his dreams.

So we come to the last thought of all. It is simply that the gift which we give to God, the divine need to which we respond, the simple offering of ourselves that we make, is used of God in ways beyond all human comprehension. John's simple baptism of water opens the heavens for Jesus and heralds the beginning of His glorious, redemptive ministry. Jeremiah's preaching saves the soul of a nation and reveals endless vistas of new truth. Peter's simple frank love for Christ lays the foundations of a Church against which all hell's legions can never prevail.

This is the greatest amazement of all. Yet remembering Who it is that takes our gifts and lives into His hand, surely we ought not to wonder but only to rejoice? "If God be for us, who can be against us?" When God accepts our lives, as He always does

when we give them, the wonder would be if miraculous
things did not happen.

But they always do. A few small loaves become a
feast for a multitude. A simple sacrament of water
unlocks the gates of heaven. A loving heart becomes a
royal throne for the Mighty God, the Everlasting
Father, the Prince of Peace. This indeed is the wonder of wonders, and yet we can all share in it and
share to the utmost if we but give what we have and
surrender what we are.

> Thou dost the strength to workman's arm impart;
> From Thee the skilled musician's mystic art,
> The grace of poet's pen or painter's hand
> To teach the loveliness of sea and land.
>
> Then grant us, Lord, in all things Thee to own,
> To dwell within the shadow of Thy throne,
> To speak and work, to think, and live, and move,
> Reflecting Thine own nature, which is love;
>
> That so, by Christ redeemed from sin and shame,
> And hallowed by Thy Spirit's cleansing flame,
> Ourselves, our work, and all our powers may be
> A sacrifice acceptable to Thee.[1]

[1] Ernest Edward Dugmore, "Almighty Father of all things
that be".

THE POWER OF HIS RESURRECTION

XVII

RISEN !

He is risen.

Sᴛ. Mᴀᴛᴛʜᴇᴡ 28:6 - Sᴛ. Mᴀʀᴋ 16:6 - Sᴛ. Lᴜᴋᴇ 24:6, 34.

"Hᴇ ɪs ʀɪsᴇɴ!" How often these words were uttered on that first Easter Morning, it is impossible to say, but certainly they passed from lip to lip and heart to heart like wildfire. They transfigured the disciples; electrified the Chief Priests; startled and amazed all who heard them.

It was the women who had heard them first. They had come, as day was breaking, carrying spices to anoint the body of their Lord and there in the place of His burial were met by an angel of light from whose lips they heard the news, "He is risen!" "With fear and great joy", we are told, they ran back to tell the disciples, bursting into the Upper Room where Peter and John had their lodging and poured out their news: "He is risen!" It did not take those two men long to reach the Garden, and pushing their way into the empty tomb, they marked the grave clothes lying in those peculiar folds, which suggested at once the triumph of their Lord. "He is risen!" they told each other, and half an hour later were telling Andrew and James, Philip and Nathaniel, and the rest.

All that day the words went winging from friend to friend and follower to follower. Young John Mark heard the whisper of them and told his mother, Mary. Someone found Joseph of Arimathea and he broke the glad tidings to Nicodemus. "He is risen!" Disciples slipped on their sandals and ran down the street to tell an acquaintance. Women put aside household tasks and went next door to break the news to a neighbour. Even children carried hurriedly scrawled notes to a friend or relative. "He is risen!"

In the seclusion of the High Priest's palace, an echo of it was heard. Early that morning, a little group of trembling, terrorized soldiers stood before Caiaphas and told in broken, halting words an incredible story of an earthquake, an open tomb, a risen Christ. Caiaphas, aided and abetted by his father-in-law, Annas, did his best to bully them out of this utterly silly and ridiculous report. But they made little headway. The superstitious fools stuck to their story and at last had their lips sealed by a substantial bribe. It would be disaster indeed, if the report ever got abroad that the Galilean was alive!

So the whisper grew until it became a great chorus ending in a mighty triumphant chant, a glorious, throbbing, thrilling song of tumultuous joy and gladness. "He is risen!" "He is risen!" "He is risen!" No three words in human history have ever counted for more than these words. Without doubt, they altered the whole destiny of man and literally turned the world upside down.

Nineteen hundred years after that first Easter Morning, they still remain supremely significant, and I personally can think of no message which this troubled, tortured race of ours needs more today than just to know that Christ is risen. "He is risen!" Whisper that news into the ears of parents and wives whose sons and husbands lie dead in a million nameless graves across the wide world. Whisper it to the desolate, desperate, defeated peoples of Europe and of Asia.

Send it out on the wings of the wind to the uttermost parts of the earth where men still sit in darkness and under the shadow of death. "He is risen!" Here is our hope and comfort, our shield and shelter, our rock and refuge in all the storms of this mortal life.

For one thing, we have here our only certain and secure safeguard as we face up to the appalling fact and the pitiless fury of evil. Since Christ is risen, evil is forever doomed. However you think of evil, whether you think of it as embodied in a personal devil, or as the spirit of rebellion against God in the human heart, its methods of attacking goodness are always the same. It begins by attempting to corrupt the good, to make the good bad. Then, when it discovers that true goodness is incorruptible, it seeks to destroy it in death. The cross and the gallows and the grave remain its final hope of victory, and to these awful things it resorts with dire relentlessness.

That was the horror of Calvary. There on that tree the evil hiding in the hearts of ordinary men sought to destroy utterly the only perfectly holy and good Being the world has ever known, the spotless Lamb of God. The chief priests and religious leaders, the representatives of Roman law and order, those pilgrims who had come to the sacred festival of the Passover, they had no intention of being party to such a crime as this. Yet the evil within their hearts was such that without knowing it, they became partners in the darkest deed of all time, the crucifixion of the Son of God.

In our own day and generation something very similar has been happening. During the past decades, we have watched so-called Christian nations become co-partners in such crimes as half a century ago would have shocked and horrified their consciences to the core. But confronted as they were by peoples determined to do justly and love mercy, they have rummaged hell to find tortures that would destroy them. Above all, they have exalted death, and chosen the grave as their path of victory. How typical of evil! It always counts upon death, the death of the good, as its final trump card, its surest weapon of conquest.

But is it? Surely the good news of Easter Day is that it is not so! "He is risen"—the Christ of God! Neither He nor His can be destroyed, and over Him and His the grave is forever powerless. They thought to destroy Him by nailing Him to a Cross and sealing Him in a tomb: but instead the darkest deed of evil has set Him free and given Him power such as wickedness has never known! On Good Friday, our Lord was imprisoned in the body and chained in human bonds: but on Easter Morning, He stood immortal and incorruptible, above time and space, omnipotent, omniscient and omni-present, eternal as God is eternal!

So it must always be. Christ, the crucified, is risen! "The blood of the martyrs becomes the seed of the Church."[1] The resurrection of Christ, if it means anything, means the eternal triumph of good over evil, the glorious victory of God over the devil. Remember that in this evil world. Remember it when, like Faust, you too are tempted to sell your soul to Satan!

Secondly, the fact that Christ is risen means that many of those experiences of life which appeared to us once as the blackest tragedy are by the grace of God transfigured into glorious triumphs. For our Lord by

[1] Tertullian.

His death and resurrection has taken the sting from death and victory from the grave.

We live in a world tense with the tragedy of suffering and of sorrow. Expressing his sympathy in the Canadian House of Commons on the loss of a great Liberator transport plane which was bringing to Canada representatives of the British Air Ministry, one of the members of the House remarked on the strange fact that so many go through all the terrors of warfare and then perish in some such accident as this. "But this," he went on, "is war".[1] The real truth is that this is life. "In the midst of life we are in death".[2] Looking back across my own ministry, there has certainly not been a month and hardly a week in which I have not had to share in some sorrow, or stand by and watch some dark tragedy harrowing the hearts of the children of men.

We have dead sorrows and living sorrows, the sorrows marked by simple crosses in some quiet God's acre, and the sorrows we must needs keep secretly at home or at least hide within our hearts. For one it is the tragedy of death, the death of the beloved. For another it is the tragedy of life, the beloved life crippled and broken, alive but yet dead. War, of course, has vastly increased these tragedies, making Easter Day dawn on a multitude of desolate homes and broken hearts. Yet this awful harvest can never make sorrow commonplace, never at least for those who suffer, never for Rachel mourning for her children, nor for Naomi lamenting the bitter loss of her husband, nor for David grieving for his friend and his son!

[1] J. H. Blackmore in House of Commons, Ottawa, 28th March, 1945.
[2] The Book of Common Prayer.

We may not speak much of these things and try to meet the passing world with a smile. Yet how dark it is for multitudes of the children of men! "I am stripped of all my honours," wrote the great Burke after his son's death, "I am torn up by the roots and lie prostrate on the earth. I am alone. I have none to meet my enemies in the gate."[1] How many others could make a like confession?

Yet are we alone? Have we no one who will meet the enemy for us in the gate? This is Easter morning and Christ is risen! By His rising again, He has transfigured and transformed all life's tragedies so that though we mourn, we mourn not as those who have no hope but as those who have all hope. Seen against the background of this world, death and disease, sorrow and suffering are meaningless, utterly insoluble. But see them against the further horizons of eternity, see them in the light of Easter Morning and they become transfigured. Because Christ rose triumphant over death and the grave, we know that though "weeping may endure for a night, joy cometh in the morning."[2] We know that death is no dark way, no dread path, but the road to life and light and immortality.

The light of Easter means the light of heaven upon the tragedies of this life. It means that "God shall wipe away all tears from their eyes; and there shall be no more death, neither sorrow nor crying, neither shall there be any more pain: for the former things are passed away."[3] In the light of Easter, you and I who carry the cross of sorrow within our hearts can with

[1] Edmund Burke, quoted by Arthur Mee *One Thousand Beautiful Things*. Hodder & Stoughton Ltd.

[2] Psalm 30:5.

[3] Revelation 21:4.

Adelaide Anne Procter lift up our heads and dry our
eyes and sing in triumph:

> I thank Thee more that all our joy
> Is touched with pain,
> That shadows fall on brightest hours,
> That thorns remain,
> So that earth's bliss may be our guide,
> And not our chain.[1]

"He is risen!" Thirdly, that glorious message not
only brings assurance of the transfiguration of life's
tragedies and the doom of its evil; it also proclaims
triumph for tomorrow. It brings promise for the future
and guarantees God and goodness for the days to
come.

No one looking out upon the world of our day can
do so with any kind of sanguine hope. For one thing
the smoking fires of war still obscure our vision. The
ultimate destruction and devastation have been even
more terrible than we feared. One thing is certain: for
many long years to come the way of life is going to be
hard and the road fraught with dread dangers for every
man, woman and child alive.

But there is hope, for Christ is risen! He is alive
and in the midst of the world. He walks the highways
of earth and has life to give to all who will receive it.
The late C. F. Andrews has told how in 1932 he spent
Easter Day in Delhi. "A gloom was over the land," he
wrote. "Wherever I went, from one Indian home to
another, the sense of impotence was mingled with
despair. Hopelessness seemed to be settling down on
the face of the earth." It was the beginning of the

---

[1] Adelaide Anne Proctor, "My God I thank Thee".

heat, and the monsoon rains were still far off. "Nature seemed to speak of decay and death." Then on Easter morning, he went to Communion, and there came to him this message, "Christ is risen! Christ is risen!"[1] Here was the news that India needed! Here was the message for the land he loved from the Lord he loved. Stronger and stronger grew the conviction that the Risen Christ could save India and could lead her out from the enveloping darkness into the fullness of life that it was His to give.

I do not despair of the future. Who can, when Christ lives? Surely in the very greatness of the events of these present tumultuous days, we must trace His handiwork and mark His footprints.

He hath sounded forth the trumpet that shall never call
    retreat:
He is sifting out the hearts of men before His judgment-
    seat;
O, be swift, my soul, to answer Him; be jubilant, my feet!
    Our God is marching on.[2]

"I go before you into Galilee" was the message He gave on that first Easter morning to His friends, and the last promise that came from Him before He ascended was the promise that He would be with us alway even unto the end of the world, "the words of a Gentleman of the strictest and most sacred honour" was how David Livingstone described them in his diary.

Yes, He goes before us, and remains with us. He leads and guides and orders all things for our good. Tomorrow and tomorrow and tomorrow you will find

[1] C. F. Andrews, *Christ in the Silence*. Hodder & Stoughton Ltd.

[2] Julia Ward Howe, "Mine eyes have seen the glory".

Him out there on the highways of life making the
rough places plain and the crooked straight, making
the wilderness glad and the desert rejoice and blossom
as the rose.

He is coming like the glory of the morning on the wave;
He is wisdom to the mighty; He is succour to the brave;
So the world shall be His footstool, and the soul of time
     His slave:
  Our God is marching on![1]

One final thought. For those first disciples Easter
Morning began with the declaration of a fact; it ended
with the proclamation of an experience. "He is risen!"
was the message that passed from lip to lip as the sun
rose over Jerusalem on that first day of the week, but
ere it set another, more wonderful message was running
like wildfire through the city. "I have seen the Lord!"
they were saying. "I have seen the Lord!" cried Mary
Magdalene as she burst into the Upper Room with the
light of heaven on her face. "I have seen the Lord!"
cried Cleopas hot with the dust of the Emmaus road
on his sandals. "I have seen the Lord!" they were all
saying before the day was dead.

And that is the real Easter, to find Christ for ourselves and find Him alive; to touch Christ and talk
with Him; to know Christ and the power of His resurrection, not simply because others have told us of Him,
but because He has come to us and we to Him. "He is
risen!" We believe that, but have we seen the Lord?
Have we found the Saviour of the World, our Saviour?

[1] Ibid.

XVIII

EASTER CLOTHES

If ye then be risen with Christ, seek those things
which are above . . . Put off the old man. . . . Put on
the new.

COLOSSIANS 3:1, 9, 10.

NOT THE LEAST attraction about Easter Sunday for
many of us lies in the fact that it spells Easter clothes.
Winter lies behind us, warmer brighter days are to
come. Away go old heavy coats and thick warm
dresses, and out comes all the finery with which we look
forward to greeting the sunshine of another summer!

Now Easter clothes are important, far more important than even the most clothes-conscious girl could
believe possible.

> At Easter let your clothes be new,
> Or else be sure you will it rue,—

runs an old rhyme. Nature herself sees to it that she
puts on new clothes at this great glad season of the
year. Every bough and branch and forest glade is
shaking out a new garment of loveliness with which to
brighten the coming days. It would be strange indeed
if we who are at least in part the children of Nature
did not follow suit.

We are, however, more than children of Nature;
we are children of God. It is for this reason primarily
that we should clothe ourselves in new garments at
Eastertide. That, indeed, is the whole burden of St.
Paul's message in this third chapter of Colossians. In

the closing verses of the second and the opening verses of the third chapter, he dwells upon the great central message of Easter. Christ Jesus, our Lord, has died for us and has risen again from the dead. There is the central fact of history, the turning point of time, an event with the most momentous of all consequences. For, argues St. Paul, the resurrection of Jesus means that death is now behind us instead of before us. Christ has died for us, and in His resurrection we have the resurrection of all who put their faith and trust in Him as Lord and God. Because of what happened on Calvary and in the Garden of the Resurrection, it is possible for all men here and now to live the full life of the sons of God. Death, not merely physical death, but the moral and spiritual death which alone can destroy immortal souls, is done with; is behind us forever, if Jesus Christ is accepted in humble faith and love as Saviour and Lord.

A tremendous declaration this, and the whole New Testament echoes with the glory of it. Death is swallowed up in victory. In Christ we have died to sin and been raised again to righteousness. Because of what He has done, here and now we are new creatures, living the full rich life of the sons of God.

But are we? That's the rub, and that is where Easter clothes come in. For, says St. Paul, if you have been raised with Christ then you must seek the things that are above, and this transformation and transfiguration of life will be evident in two things. It will be seen in the clothes we have put off: and it will be made clear by the clothes we have put on.

Our new life will be evident from the clothes we have put off. The Apostle goes on to detail these

clothes that must be discarded. First of all we must
put off the clothes of immorality and impurity, of
passion, evil desire, and covetousness. It goes without
saying, he argues, that these must be put off. In fact
they must be utterly destroyed; they must be put to
death; for these are nothing less than the clothes of
death. They bind the soul of man to the sensual and
temporal. They crush the spirit and narrow it down
until it becomes a mere appendage to the body. These
clothes must be destroyed, for no one who has been
born again to newness of life will ever think of wearing
them.

Have we, then, put away forever these fleshly grave
clothes of lust and passion, these awful shrouds that
once held our souls in bondage? Or are we still clinging
to them, hiding them beneath the gay finery with
which we have decked ourselves? Perhaps we put
them off only to keep them locked away in some secret
place whence, from time to time, we bring them forth
and sport ourselves in their obscenities? Honesty with
ourselves is a cardinal virtue. We have not all destroyed
those evil things. The books that are best sellers on
our bookstalls make that plain. The picture magazines
lying around our homes testify against us. The amusements we seek out bear a like witness. We want the
grace and salvation and liberty of the Christ-life. Yet
we cling miserably to these rags of shame. Had we not
better, this Eastertide, put off these old clothes, and so
cleanse the imaginations of our hearts that Jesus Christ
may live in us and we in Him?

St. Paul goes on to give another list of garments
that must be put off before we can put on the new man.
There is anger and wrath, malice and slander and all
foul talk. After the sins of the flesh come the sins of

the spirit, and it is instructive to note just what these
sins are. Anger first, for anger is the spiritual equiva-
lent of murder. He who is angry with his brother,
said Jesus, is in danger of hell fire. Yet how often we
allow anger to have its way with us! How easily
tempers are raised, tongues loosened, and the whole
bitterness of our souls poured forth in contempt of
our brother! Press far enough, says St. Paul, and you
find that anger and wrath lead on to malice and slander, to all kinds of foul talk and lying lips. Life instead
of being a cosmos, an ordered unity, becomes a chaos
with each man set against his brother, and society dis-
integrating into conflicting groups which can never
hope to win any kind of peace.

Look at the nations and society. Here is Greek
maligning Jew and Jew despising Greek. Here are the
religious and privileged mocking the irreligious and
non-privileged. Here is nation divided against nation,
class against class. What a tragedy it all is, and what
crimes are committed in the names of justice and
brotherhood and God! Yet it all follows from those
garments of superiority and selfishness with which the
old man has clothed himself. It comes from the sin of
judging others in hot anger or cold calculating malice,
from hasty searing selfish criticism and the sowing
broadcast of lies. Certainly this is not the world as
God planned it, but the world as man's sin and selfishness have defaced it. It is a world that breeds wars
and rumours of wars, not a world where life goes on to
become more and more abundant.

How vital, then, that we who are raised with Christ
should put off the old man! For the sake of our own
souls we must do this thing, taking off and finally de-
stroying the garments of sensual lusts and passions.

And for the sake of society, we must take off the spiritual habiliments of pride and anger and evil speaking. We must guard our lips as well as our imaginations, and see the world and mankind as God saw them in the beginning, "renewed in knowledge after the image of the creator", "one in Christ Jesus."

With what clothes then are we to dress ourselves, we who are Christ's and have been raised from death with Christ? St. Paul gives a full list of them in this third chapter. We who are "God's chosen ones, holy and beloved", must put on compassion and kindness, lowliness and meekness, patience, forbearance, and a forgiving spirit. Above all we must put on love which binds everything together in perfect harmony.

We are to put off passion, the passion that uses others as chattels and put on compassion that feels for others as our brothers in Christ. We are to put off the pride that blazes forth in anger and clothe ourselves in kindness, lowliness, meekness. We are in a word, to go among men as servants, not as masters, finding life's greatest joy in doing good to them and for them. Then of course there must be patience, for the kingdom of God cannot come in a day nor an hour. We shall have to exercise also a great forbearance and a forgiving spirit to undergird our brother man where he fails and falters. Supreme over all let there be love, love which is the cement of character, and the crowning robe of the spirit's immortal dress.

What can be said about this dress? This first, that it is the most distinctive and attractive dress in the wide world. A dress worth wearing must at least be attractive, and what distinction and attraction this dress has given to men. No one would ever have heard

of the Bedford tinker had he not put on Christ Jesus,
but having put off the old and put on the new he found
immortality. That has been true all down the centuries.
Who would have heard of David Livingstone, or Dr.
Grenfell, of Lord Shaftesbury or Florence Nightingale,
of Henry Drummond or D. L. Moody, of Dr. Aggrey
or Booker Washington had they not put off the old man
and put on the new?

There is nothing less attractive than the dress of
worldliness. It levels us down and hides personality.
It regiments us in the drabest of all uniforms. But
this Easter robe which Christ gives to His own not
only always attracts but always reveals the latent gifts
and talents and graces of those who put it on. A little
railway clerk put it on some seventy years ago and
became John McNeill the world-famous evangelist.
Robert Browning put it on and it made him the
greatest modern Christian poet. A backwoodsman's
son put it on and became the greatest President of the
United States of America. There is nothing that can
add such distinction to life as this dress. Go on wearing
the old rags of worldliness and we will continue to be
nobodies. But put on Jesus Christ and at once we
become somebody, somebody attractive, distinctive.

Then again this Easter dress which Christ offers
is by far the most durable. It never wears, never grows
old or threadbare or shabby. Indeed, it is the only
dress that improves with the wearing, for the longer
you wear it, the finer it becomes and the lovelier it
appears to those who see it. You begin with compassion and meekness and you end with love and the
peace of Christ dwelling in you richly. You begin with
kindness and lowliness and you end with thankfulness,
doing everything in the name of the Lord Jesus. The

world's clothes grow threadbare and at the last they leave us naked and helpless, but these Easter clothes of our Lord last on for ever. Neither time, nor tide, nor the swelling of Jordan can take them from us, and in glory they shall shine as the light itself.

Put off the old. . . . Put on the new.

Have we put off the old and put on the new? Have we died with Christ and risen with Him to newness of life? Is death forever behind us and are we facing to-morrow clothed in all the righteousness of God?

At Easter let your clothes be new
Or else be sure you will it rue.

XIX

THE CONQUEST OF THE SAVAGE

The wolf also shall dwell with the lamb.

ISAIAH 11:6.

IN THE WHOLE animal kingdom there is no more terrible and persistent family than that of the wild dog, and king of this galloping host is the unconquerable wolf. Civilization has advanced against him with all its armour, but still "he remains a splendid and terrible savage", assured of his place "by reason of his audacity, his cunning, his ability to front adversity and counter changing conditions with new tactics". The result is that today the wolf continues as a menace and a terror in lands where the arts of peace have flourished for two thousand years and more.

Just after the first world war, in 1921, wolves spread terror through the Moselle district of France, while great packs swarmed across the plains of Italy. That same winter, Rumanian wolves in one night killed five peasants and injured thirty others, while of Russia and Asia a whole literature of tragedy could be written on lives sacrificed to make a feast for wolves. "The cold and the darkness make me afraid. Let us shelter in one of those cottages whose lights I see," said Miss Marsden, an English missionary to the driver as she sledged through the Russian night. "Madame," came the answer, "these are not lights in cottage windows. These are the eyes of wolves."[1]

It is amazing how persistent the wolf has been. All

[1] *The Children's Encyclopedia*, Vol. I, "The Wild Dogs".

over Europe, with the exception of Britain and Northern Germany; over wide areas of Russia; throughout the greater part of Asia and North America, the wolf clings to life, the fiercest and in many ways the most deadly of the denizens of the animal kingdom. Yet, it is this animal, this untamed ravenous beast of prey, which Isaiah pictures as dwelling at peace with the lamb, the gentlest, the most defenceless, the most innocent of God's creatures! How can such a thing ever happen and such a vision find fulfilment?

Isaiah was of course dreaming of the day when the knowledge of God would cover the earth as the waters cover the sea. He was seeing in imagination the Kingdom of Heaven as it would appear upon the earth, and the kernel of that message was simply that all the wild, brutal, murderous forces of life, those forces of which the wolf and the leopard, the lion and the bear, are typical examples, are to be tamed and harnessed, until one day they take their place alongside all of virtue and of grace, of truth and of beauty. "The wolf shall dwell with the lamb, and the leopard shall lie down with the kid." A glorious vision indeed, but what hope is there of its ever being realized?

Before seeking to answer that question, look more closely at the vision itself. "The wolf also shall dwell with the lamb." There is an Italian proverb which runs, "The death of the wolf is the health of the sheep",[1] but obviously that was not Isaiah's view, nor the objective which Isaiah's God had set before Himself. There is no question here of eliminating the wolf; instead his powers are to be sublimated. The problem which the wolf presents is not to be solved by his

[1] John Florio, *First Fruits*.

destruction but by his discipline; not by annihilation but by assimilation. From being a danger to life, he is to be transformed into a fit partner for life, a suitable and trustworthy companion for the innocent and innocuous lamb.

This possibility is frequently overlooked by religious people when they are faced with the problem of dealing with the wolf in life. How often, in recent years, have good people wished earnestly that God would intervene and remove from the European arena some of those wolves who have so troubled the peace of mankind. Just before the Second World War, Mr. Vernon Bartlett gave expression to this deep desire when he remarked that "the world will know no peace until Franco's widow tells Stalin on his deathbed of the assassination of Hitler at Mussolini's funeral." Exactly! We want to exterminate the whole breed from life, and then we believe we shall have peace. Peace! I wonder if peace would best describe such a state? Might stagnation not be nearer the truth?

The foolishness of God is wiser than men, and well He knows how infinitely poorer and weaker, more colourless and spineless life would be were the wolf to be destroyed. For He has created the wolf as well as the lamb; He brought to birth the leopard as well as the kid; He fashioned the poisonous asp as well as the little child. Moreover He did so because the energies and powers of these creatures are somehow valuable and necessary for a full and rich life. They have their own distinctive contribution to make to the total well-being of creation, and only the misdirection of their powers is evil.

There, I suggest, is a not inadequate definition of sin. Sin is simply the misdirection of valuable powers and energies; the using of a good thing for an evil end; the perversion of noble instincts; the harnessing of high and heavenly powers to low ideals and sordid purposes. The ferocity of the wolf, for example, can be a devilish thing, when, as happened a few years ago in Afghanistan, one mad wolf bit and destroyed in a single night seventy-eight camels.[1] Yet no one would deny a mother wolf her ferocity in defending her defenceless cubs against the attack of a leopard or a bear.

So it is in human life. The pugnacious instinct in man, to take one example, that deep urge to prove our strength in battle, is altogether evil when it is directed towards the destruction of defenceless cities and the wholesale slaughter of helpless women and children. Yet without that same instinct we could hardly have the chivalry and daring of the reformers who have battled for social justice and spiritual liberty. Slay this wolf of pugnacity, and you destroy one of life's greatest driving forces, one of the mightiest energies for the transformation and salvation of humanity.

Yet how many have asked God to do this very thing within their lives? We have prayed that He would take from us one or other of the great instinctive forces which have raged through our lives like ravening wolves. Men have asked to be delivered from an ungoverned temper, from a strong sexual passion, from an overweening ambition. But our prayers get negative answers. God refuses to amputate these limbs of the spirit. His will is not the destruction of the wolf but the disciplining of the wolf; not the annihilation of life's strong, terrible powers, but their sublimation for higher and holier purposes. "The wolf also shall dwell with the lamb." For only when that dream has been

---

[1] *The Children's Encyclopedia*, Vol. 1, "The Wild Dogs".

realized can the Kingdom of God become an accomplished fact within our lives and within the world at large. Only then shall the knowledge of God cover the earth as the waters cover the sea, and nothing hurt or destroy in all His Holy Mountain.[1]

But how is this transformation of life's savage and untamed forces to take place? Isaiah's conviction was that it would be accomplished by a God-inspired Man, enlightened, patient, working with wisdom and righteousness. The Messiah Himself would bring about this miracle of discipline and harmony. The Christ would have power to conquer and control life's wild unconquered powers. Two things in particular need to be noted in this gospel proclaimed by the prophet.

In the first place, it is God Himself who is to take the initiative in conquering the wolf and the leopard. That fact needs emphasis and re-emphasis today; for so often we leave God out of count and act as though He had no actual existence. Again and again during these past years we have talked and thought and acted as though the destiny of our race lay in the hands of a few men who had risen to exalted state. Humanity has seemed to us to lie at the mercy of their slightest whim. No wonder there has been unrest abroad! No wonder we have lived panic-stricken as though on top of a volcano!

Such an attitude must always be unworthy of Christian people. For it is nothing less than a denial of our faith as disciples, and evidence of our complete lack of understanding of the things of the Spirit. God is still in His heaven; He is still the Ruler and Governor of this universe, and nothing can happen in it without

[1] Isaiah 11:9.

at least the consent of His will. That does not mean that life is not dangerous, and will not continue to remain dangerous. But it does mean that come what may,—joy or sorrow, peace or further war, the dissolution of our civilization or the consolidation of it, God will continue to be in final and absolute control. God will reign and in the end He will make all things work together for the good of them that love Him.

Let us remember that the curbing and taming of the wolf and the leopard are His Self-ordained tasks. In creating them, He has made Himself responsible for them, and He alone has the power one day to make "the wolf dwell with the lamb and the leopard lie down with the kid".

Secondly, we need to note the special instrument which God has chosen for the fulfilment of this vast divine undertaking. He has chosen none other than His own son, Jesus Christ, "Who was conceived by the Holy Ghost, born of the Virgin Mary: suffered under Pontius Pilate, was crucified, dead, and buried".[1] Divinely inspired, enlightened and guided by His Father's Spirit, and armed with the strength of righteousness, our Lord has to prove Himself equal to this stupendous undertaking. It sounds an unpromising way by which to overcome the forces of darkness and tame the wolf of lawlessness, but thanks be to God "the foolishness of God is wiser than men; and the weakness of God is stronger than men."[2]

We are slow indeed to believe, yet history and experience are constantly preaching that love is

[1] *The Apostle's Creed.*
[2] I Corinthians 1:25.

mightier than hate; that mind is master over matter; that understanding is lord over brute force. The very dog that lies on the hearth rug, that licks your hand in affection and runs before you down the road, is irrefutable evidence of this fact; for he is blood brother to the wolf, this most faithful and loyal of man's animal friends! Ages ago our prehistoric ancestors took him a cub from the wolf's lair, and by determined, persistent, patient discipline and love succeeded in turning these savage instincts into new and useful channels. The result is that today the wolf not only dwells with the lamb, but has become the very guardian of the lamb. Wisdom has mastered wickedness; intelligence triumphed over instinct; love won the day over hate.

In the kingdom of human relationships and on the plane of human experience, it is no different. There too the unseen outlives the seen, and the love of Christ constrains us. Centuries ago that love, clothed in the simple habit of wandering friars, broke down the barriers of race and tribe within the land of our fathers, uniting Angle and Briton, Pict and Scot into one strong nation. Today the same miracle is manifest across vast areas of Africa, Asia and America. Tomorrow it will find fulfilment across the whole earth.

Indeed, I believe that our children's children will look back and marvel at the folly and blindness and evil of this generation; at its colossal waste of its resources in armaments; at its debasing debaucheries of war. For these children will have seen east and west, north and south, Nazi and Communist and Democrat dwell together as children of the one Father and brothers of the one Lord. They will have seen "the wolf dwell with the lamb, and the leopard lie down with the kid". That is no beautiful idyllic dream, but the Word of the Living God to this generation.

Again in human experience how true it is that "the love of Christ constraineth us" and that "the Lamb of God taketh away the sin of the world"! There are countless men and women around us today who are witnesses of this fact; who know that they would not be here and would not be occupying their place of responsibility in life, were it not for the redeeming grace of God. He has done so much for us! He has saved us from so many pitfalls, and kept us from so many disasters. The wolf in us has been curbed, if not converted, to new positive service; the leopard has been held, if not harnessed, to the higher purposes of life. And the secret of it all has been that the strong hand of Christ has been upon us. He and He alone has kept "my soul from death, mine eyes from tears, and my feet from falling".[1]

Curbed but not converted! Held but not harnessed! How true that is for so many! The wolf within is caged and the leopard in chains. But God wants to do much more than this for us. Through Christ He seeks to set us gloriously free. He wants to let loose a hundred new and glorious powers that today are imprisoned by the wolf and the leopard, so that the most mediocre might become outstanding and the weakest strong. His motto for our lives is not repression, but expression! Not the binding of the wolf, but the disciplining and harnessing of his energies for a higher and holier service both here and hereafter!

[1] Psalm 116:8.

What an opportunity is this, and what a chance to become the person we have so long wanted to become! Let God have His way with us. "Commit thy ways unto the Lord and He shall direct thy paths." Then indeed, "the wolf shall dwell with the lamb and the leopard shall lie down with the kid. . . . And the earth shall be full of the knowledge of the Lord, as the waters cover the sea."

XX

WHERE ARE OUR DEAD?

They shall be His people, and God Himself shall be
with them and be their God. And God shall wipe
away all tears from their eyes; and there shall be no
more death, neither sorrow, nor crying, neither shall
there be any more pain: for the former things are
passed away.

REVELATION 21:3-4.

WHERE are our dead? Hardly a week passes but a
minister finds himself in some house with darkened
windows and sorrowful hearts. Hardly a week passes
but death casts its dark mantle over some life that we
have known and perhaps loved. Where then have they
gone? Where is that boy who sat beside us in the
schoolroom; that lad who worked with us at our bench;
that neighbour whose presence gave life a special fine-
ness and nobility; that dear one whose hands were so
gentle and whose heart was so great in its love?

I think of the friends who are dead, who were dear long ago
     in the past,
Beautiful friends who are dead, though I know that death
     cannot last;
Friends with the beautiful eyes that the dust has defiled,
Beautiful souls who were gentle when I was a child.[1]

Yes, where are they all? Where are our dead?

In considering this question, there is one danger

[1] John Masefield, *Collected Poems* - "Twilight". Wm. Heinemann Ltd.

against which we must guard. A friend once told me of meeting an Orkney farmer whose minister the previous Sunday had been preaching on the subject of Heaven. "And what is Heaven like?" asked my friend. "Man," came the disgusted answer, "he told us it was just like the east mainland of Orkney."

This incident illustrates an error which at all costs we must avoid in our consideration of this great question, the error of claiming a knowledge we do not possess and detail that is impossible. Indeed, the Canon of Windsor, Dr. Anthony Deane, in his book on this subject declares that "there are only two conclusions at which we can safely arrive. One is that while we remain on earth we shall always wonder but never know. And the other is that the fact that we do not know is really quite unimportant."[1]

The truth is that our knowledge of life after death is necessarily limited and fragmentary and that for this reason: life hereafter is qualitatively different from life as we experience it on earth. It is not simply that when we die we continue to live, but we begin to live an entirely different kind of life, a life so different from anything that we have known here in time that we cannot possibly conceive what it is really like.

Take for example one of the obvious differences between the life that the dear dead are living and our life. Here on this side of reality, we find ourselves imprisoned within the walls of a material body, a body that is the instrument of God in the education and discipline of our spirits. But the dead know no such limitation. They are free from the shackles of a material frame. St. Paul tells us that they have a

---

[1] Anthony C. Deane, *The Valley and Beyond*. Hodder & Stoughton Ltd.

"spiritual body".[1] Spiritualists speak of an "astral body": but one thing is certain, that body is not limited by time or place. It is free as the birds are free. It is the music that persists when the violin has been broken. It is the flower that blooms in the light when the bulb that gave it birth lies rotting in the earth.

Obviously, then, we who have never known any life outside this body cannot envisage a life that is free from such anchorage. But that is the life that our dead are living, a life of which none of us have or can have any experience on this earthly plane, a life that we can only dimly apprehend through the medium of symbols and figures. Nevertheless, it is a life which will be as natural to us when we reach it as is this world into which we have come through the strange process of birth.

The experience of death must indeed be very similar to the experience of birth. Before birth we knew nothing of the universe into which we were coming. Had it been possible for those about us to communicate with us in that dark pre-natal world of our conception, could we have understood their descriptions of this world with its morning and evening, its light and shadow, its beauty and truth, its love and goodness? You know we could never have understood them, for we had no concepts adequate to grasp the richness of human experience. It is the same with the great Beyond. We cannot know. We have no language, no experience to understand or appreciate the World of Eternity in which our dead live.

The Christian Gospel has put this truth in another way. Our knowledge is limited, says the New Testa-

[1] I Corinthians 15:44.

ment, because life after death is so much more wonderful, so vastly more glorious than life as we know it here. We cannot know because the description of it beggars imagination. "Eye hath not seen, nor ear heard, neither have entered into the heart of man, the things which God hath prepared for them that love Him."[1]

> High is the rank we now possess;
>   But higher we shall rise;
> Though what we shall hereafter be
>   Is hid from mortal eyes;
> Our souls, we know, when He appears,
>   Shall bear His image bright;
> For all His glory, full disclosed,
>   Shall open to our sight.[2]

Translate that into plain language and it means that the life to come is so wonderful, so glorious, so sublime that it must be experienced to be known. It is not too good to be true; but too good not to be true!

Turn then to this great question, "Where are our Dead?" and let us try to find within the limitation of our knowledge if any answer is possible to it. There are, I believe, three convictions we can hold with the utmost certainty,—three truths which come to us out of the pages of Scripture and out of the living pages of human experience.

The first is that our dead are near to God and with God. One of the main articles of the Christian faith is that God is not only transcendent, above and be-

[1] I Corinthians 2:9.
[2] Scottish Paraphrases, 1781, vv. 3-4.

yond all the work of His creation; but He is also immanent, omnipresent, in all things and through all things. "If I ascend up into heaven, thou art there: if I make my bed in hell, behold, thou art there."[1]

Remembering this, it would hardly be true to say that our dead are nearer to God than we are. Yet there is a sense in which this is true, for our dead know they are near to God. To paraphrase St. Paul's words we can say: "You and I see through a glass, darkly; but they see face to face. We know in part; but they know even as also they are known."[2]

It is this thought which St. John presents so vividly in that great vision of the New Jerusalem which he has given us in the Book of Revelation. He tells us that in the rhapsody of that hour he heard "a great Voice out of Heaven saying, Behold, the tabernacle of God is with men, and He will dwell with them, and they shall be His people, and God Himself shall be with them, and be their God."[3] Our dead are with God. They are near to Him, safe within the shelter and security of the Everlasting Arms. "Today," said Jesus to the dying thief, "shalt thou be with me in Paradise."[4]

There is comfort in that thought for all of us who have seen death rob our homes and empty our hearts. For to know our dear ones are with God is to know that they have perfect peace and fullness of joy. All of us have known someone who has lived sensitive to the Presence of God, and in every such life one cannot fail to find a serenity, a joy, a calm which the world

[1] Psalm 139:8.
[2] I Corinthians 13:12.
[3] Revelation 21:3.
[4] St. Luke 23:43.

can neither give nor take away. To be near to God here in time is to have peace. How much truer then it must be of those who dwell in the Eternal Light of that Eternal Day! They are with God and "the peace that passeth all understanding"[1] must be theirs also.

Secondly, I believe our dead have escaped the harassing limitations which bound them when here on earth. They have done with physical bonds, and that means that they have done with so much of pain and sorrow, with so many overwhelming temptations and hopeless fears. The fires of corroding passions are spent. The consuming darkness of depression and despair is ended. They dwell in light abundant and full of glory. "They shall hunger no more; neither thirst any more; neither shall the sun light on them nor any heat: for the Lamb which is in the midst of the Throne shall feed them and shall lead them unto living fountains of water: and God shall wipe away all tears from their eyes."[2] What a vision of glory that is! What a message of joy to know that our dead have escaped from all "the slings and arrows of outrageous fortune"![3]

> Safely, safely gathered in,
> No more sorrow, no more sin,
> No more childish griefs or fears,
> No more sadness, no more tears![4]

If this is death, then surely in Masefield's words, "it is most grand to die."[5]

[1] Philippians 4:7.
[2] Revelation 7:16-17.
[3] William Shakespeare, *Hamlet*, Act iii, Sc. 1.
[4] Henrietta Dobree, "Safely, safely gathered in."
[5] John Masefield, *Poems*, "Pompey The Great". Wm. Heinemann Ltd.

And if this be death, then we cannot sorrow as those who have no hope. Sorrow of course there must be when life is broken and shattered by the loss of our loved ones. Something within each of us must die when our dear ones die. But the loss is ours, not theirs. Those who remain, not those who pass on, are the poorer; and therefore if we truly love our dead, we cannot, we must not grudge them their victory and their peace. "My dear, don't call me back this time," said a friend, a great African missionary, to his wife when blackwater fever had struck him down for the second time. Before, she had called him back. She had agonized in prayer by his bedside when the doctors had given up all hope. But this time she let him go to his rest, rejoicing in the knowledge that he had won through to life abundant. We must not grudge our dear ones their rest. Selfishness can have no place in our sorrow.

> Safely, safely gathered in,
> Free from sorrow, free from sin,
> Passed beyond all grief and pain.
> Death for thee is truest gain:
> For our loss we must not weep,
> Nor our loved one long to keep
> From the home of rest and peace,
> Where all sin and sorrow cease.[1]

Finally, we can hold firmly and without doubt that those who have died are engaged in the service of God's Everlasting Kingdom, and that part of that service is to help those of us who remain behind and still love them to attain the life everlasting.

[1] Henrietta Dobree, "Safely, safely gathered in".

There is a popular misconception which pictures Heaven as a state of perpetual Sabbath rest, an endless and weary idleness and inactivity. But that is never the Rest of which the Scriptures speak. The Rest that belongs to the people of God is rest from sin, rest from fear and from all the weaknesses that have undermined our character and destroyed our peace on earth. But it is never rest from labour nor from service. Indeed, the reverse is true. For death means the setting free of ourselves, of our gifts and talents for a very much greater and more effective service. "Greater works than these shall ye do, because I go unto my Father,"[1] said Jesus. Our Lord anticipated for Himself a wider sphere of service after death than before it; and a great part of that service was to be service for His disciples.

Think then of our dead not as paralysed in a state of perpetual inactivity, but growing into a fuller, richer life. Those latent talents which remained undeveloped on earth are today finding full expression. Those half-used gifts for which time had so little place are coming into new circulation. Those personalities, dwarfed and repressed by circumstances, are blossoming forth into a wonderful richness and beauty and value in the service of the Father.

And surely part of that service must be to help those of us on this side who still hold them in loving remembrance. Indeed, if all our dead do is to quicken our memories and bring back to mind lost ideals, to create a hunger in our hearts for higher things and steel our wills to greater endurance, their service is no small thing, and this at least our beloved dead do for us. Writing of the beautiful memory which his young

[1] St. John 14:12.

mother had left, Prince Kropotkin has said: "Men passionately desire to live after death, but they often pass away without noticing the fact that the memory of a really good person always lives. It is impressed upon the next generation and is transmitted again to the children. Is not that an immortality worth striving for?"[1]

Our dead live in our memories. But they live also in other ways. We believe in the presence of Christ with us in life. Should we not also believe in the encircling presence of those "whom we have loved long since and lost awhile", of those who are with Christ? Are we, too, not "compassed about with a great cloud of witnesses"? Are our dead not watching our every movement, watching the ebb and flow of our lives, the swing of the battle, the growth of our character? I believe they are. I believe in the Communion of the Saints. I believe that death has brought no real division between ourselves and our loved ones who have gone before. "Wherefore seeing we also are compassed about with so great a cloud of witnesses, let us lay aside every weight, and the sin which doth so easily beset us, and let us run with patience the race that is set before us, looking unto Jesus the author and finisher of our faith."[2]

[1] Quoted by David Williamson in *Gathered Harvest*. Rich & Cowan.

[2] Hebrews 12:1-2.

XXI

CHRIST, THE SOVEREIGN TRUTH

"Where is he that is born King of the Jews?"

St. Matthew 2:2.

"Jesus said . . . 'I am the Truth'."

St. John 14:6.

From Bethlehem to Calvary one word kept being repeated like a whispered refrain, the word "King". Matthew Arnold tells us that in that "sad pagan world, men were looking for a king." They wanted a king to set them free from bondage, a king to break the power of tyranny, to end the miseries and frustrations and tragedies of their lives and so lead them out to possess a new heaven and a new earth. "Men were looking for a king".

And they are still looking for a king. It is true that a very large proportion of the inhabited world has allowed itself to depart from the ideal of kingship and accept some form of republican government. But that has not ended this craving for a king to rule over us. Kings have been deposed, but in their place we have set dictators and given to them such powers as kings have seldom known, such powers indeed as belong only to God.

The sum of the matter is that the human heart is so constituted that it is never happier than when giving obeisance to some one greater than itself. We are never happier than when we are under discipline and following a leader, a lord, a king. Furthermore this craving for a king becomes almost more than flesh and blood can bear when men find themselves the impotent slaves of powers against which they cannot do battle. That is why, in this modern world, with all its glorious possibilities and awful perils, men give over their liberty holus-bolus to dictators. We know ourselves to be quite inadequate to deal with the terrifying problems which confront us. We want escape. We want another to carry our cross and wear our crown.

So the need for a king persists in a world which has thought itself mature enough to abolish kingship. It continues our greatest and most vital need. Where then shall we find this king? Who will be king among us, giving rest to our souls and security to our hearts and homes? "Where is he that is born King?"

Jesus Christ is King! That was the hope which followed the Man of Nazareth down the years. It broke like dawn about His cradle at Bethlehem and startled those closest to the Child in the manger. It troubled Herod in his palace and worried his advisers. The rumour of it shadowed His path so that on more occasions than one, men would have taken and made Him king. It persisted to the bitter tragic end, for the title of "King" was above His head as He died upon the Cross.

It was wise men from the East however, who first suggested that He was King. "Where is he that is born King?" they came asking. These men of faith and vision, of scholarship and letters, whose whole lives had been spent in the most profound thought concerning God and His creation felt that the very nature of things demanded the coming of a king. The whole universe of law and order, of truth and beauty, of wisdom and love pointed to one ultimate sovereign mind and will, to one king.

For the true scholar the sovereign thing in this universe must always be truth. He must seek after truth whether the search brings him to the depths of hell or the heights of heaven. Truth is king, and only the truth can set us free. In every age scholars and thinkers, philosophers and sages, the wise and the good have believed that the truth could be found and would be revealed. "Where is he that is born King?" The men who asked that question had no doubt that the king worthy of their adoration and worship could be found. Their problem was to discover *where* He was born, where He had revealed Himself.

Again and again down the centuries the answer, which above all others has met and satisfied the intellectual and spiritual leaders of our race is that Jesus Christ is King. He is King in the realm of truth. He is God's answer to man's questioning. He is God's gift to our deep abiding human need for leadership and lordship. He is the key and solution to all the baffling problems and dark doubtings which beset this little life.

There are three areas in particular in which the kingship of Christ in the realm of truth remains unchallenged.

Take first of all the creation itself of which we are a part. How are we to understand the world about us? How are we to read its story or fathom its mystery? The universe presents us with such infinite varieties of being and of life! One thing is clear: there is order in this universe of stars and planets, of earth and ether. We live in a uni-verse. Design is apparent in all its aspects. Beauty is manifest in its myriad forms and fragments. The world is one.

But that does not answer our great questions as to how and why and whither. To what is it all leading? Where must it all end? Is there meaning and purpose, plan and pattern behind its being? It is no answer to these questions to say that man is the crown of creation. He may indeed be the crown of creation, but he is still part of creation, and may well prove to be its destroyer.

There is however one answer which, if it does not solve all the mystery, at least brings us such flooding of light that it does more than any other answer to dispel the mystery. And that answer is Christ. See the world in the light of Christ's life, and we are confronted by One whose place and power within it are unique. The world of earth and air, of sea and sky, of flowers and birds and beasts all seemed to recognize in Him their lord and master. In the wilderness of temptation wild beasts prowled about Him but not one hair of His head was hurt. He had power over all created things,—power to change stones into bread, or multiply a few small loaves and fishes into a banquet for a multitude. The winds and the waves obeyed Him. A flourishing tree withered at His word, and when at last He hung upon His cross the very heavens seemed to darken and mourn His death. Read the Gospels and the undisputed testimony which they give is that Jesus Christ was Lord and King over creation. He was always its Master, never its servant; always its King, never its subject or slave.

We may of course choose to turn our backs upon this record, and deny the tested, tried truth of the Gospel. Do that and the mystery of creation grows impenetrably dark. The universe becomes one vast unsolved riddle. On the other hand when men accept Christ as He revealed Himself and as His contemporaries knew Him, there is only one conclusion left open to us. It is that Jesus is King,—King over heaven and earth and Lord of creation. "All things," says John, "were made by Him; and without Him was not anything made that was made."[1] The whole universe is Christ's obeying His law, manifesting His glory, fulfilling His purposes.

How much we need to remember this! Arm our spirits with its truth, and nothing shall ever again make us fearful or afraid. For with Christ as King over creation, we know that "nothing can separate us from His love"; that all things are His; and that all creatures obey His holy will and fulfil His heavenly purposes. "Though the earth be removed, and though the mountains be carried into the midst of the sea; though the waters thereof roar and be troubled, yet will not we fear. For God is our refuge and strength."[2]

> "The Lord is King! lift up thy voice,
>   O earth, and all ye heavens, rejoice;
>   From world to world the joy shall ring,
>   'The Lord Omnipotent is King' ".[3]

But turn to another area of knowledge and experience in which we have great need of enlightenment and guidance. We need to know the truth about ourselves. "Know thyself" has always been regarded as one of the primary needs of this life, and today it

[1] St. John 1:3.
[2] Psalm 46:1-3.
[3] Josiah Conder, 1789-1855: "The Lord is King!"

remains among the most persistent and passionate of human desires.

In past ages men turned to the philosopher and theologian for self-knowledge. They read their Marcus Aurelius or their Epictetus. They studied Augustine or Thomas Aquinas or John Calvin, to discover what was the Christian doctrine of man. Today however the psychologist with his new insights has apparently stolen the field, and everywhere men are reading books on "How to overcome fear, or an inferiority complex", "How to be happy, or successful, or mature". The truth is that today as in all past days men confess that they do not know themselves, and are still feverishly searching for the truth about themselves.

But can we find this truth within ourselves and by ourselves? Can we pull ourselves up by our own boot laces? Must we not seek the truth beyond ourselves and above ourselves? Above all, surely if we are to know the truth about man, we must take into account the most significant and dynamic and wonderful Man who has ever lived, the Man Christ Jesus? We must see all our lives over against the example and achievements of His life. We must measure ourselves by His stature and try ourselves by His standards.

Jesus Christ is still the one absolutely unique and perfect Man in human history. No man ever spoke as He did, and no man ever lived as He did. After twenty centuries He still towers head and shoulders above the rest of us, and is without peer in the realm of human character and influence.

But how could this be? The only adequate answer to that question that has ever been given is that He is the answer to our age old question, What is Man? He is God's revelation to us of ourselves. He is the perfect pattern that we must follow, the only sure guide through time, the final and absolute authority for all the sons of men.

I remember well one bright spring afternoon driving with a well-known Professor of Psychiatry from one of our great Canadian Universities. We were talking about the modern interest in man and the hunger of so many to know themselves, as revealed by the flood of popular literature on the subject. "Within the Bible and particularly within the New Testament", said my friend, "there is far more wisdom and insight and help and guidance and truth concerning ourselves and the way of true abundant life than there is in all the books of psychology put together". What a confession for a great teacher to make! What a testimony to the sovereignty of Christ in the realm of self-knowledge! All that Freud and Jung and Adler and the rest have done has simply been to reveal the real depths of Christ's insight and knowledge of man.

To know ourselves, then, we must come to Him. We must see ourselves against the background of His life, and faith, and peace, and power, and joy. Here is life abundant, life as you and I desire to live it and as God planned that we should live it. Here too is the secret of such triumphant achievement. "I am the true and living Way",[1] He told His friends before He left them for the Cross. And now when all the centuries have rolled past, He still remains the only true and living way. Tens of thousands in our day and in every day have proved this true in their own experience. They came to Christ, they followed Christ, they obeyed Christ, they trusted Christ, and they found themselves. They became new creatures, whole creatures, the

[1] St. John 14:6.

happy, released, victorious children of God. "In him is life; and the life is the light of men".[1] See then that you walk in that light!

In conclusion, if Christ is King in the realm of nature and of human nature, if He is the Truth that illumines the mystery of creation and of character, this can only be because He is in the final analysis not man but God, not the Son of Man but the Son of God. If He is King over nature and over human nature, it is because He is King of Kings and Lord of Lords, very God of very God.

"Where is he that is born King?" All down the ages the wisest and best of men kept asking that question, for they have known that the light which shone within their own minds and hearts must have been kindled by some greater Light, and the truth, of which they caught fitful gleams, must somewhere be shining in all its eternal glory. All truly great and reverent scholars have always known that somewhere and somehow God must reveal Himself. The temporal cannot unveil the eternal, and if we are to know God, then He must take the initiative and make Himself known to us in time. So down the long centuries men have kept looking for a King, for a Messiah, for God manifest in human flesh. East and west, north and south that faith has never flickered and never failed.

Then Jesus was born in Bethlehem of Judea. From that moment to this men everywhere have been asking: "Who is this?" "Art thou the King of the Jews?" "Art thou the Messiah of God?" "Art thou the Son of God?" And from that moment to this ever increasing multitudes of our fellowmen have believed in Him, and

[1] St. John 1:4.

believing have proved to themselves that He is indeed none other than "the Word made flesh", God incarnate, God revealing Himself and thus answering the very deepest of all our human longings.

What is the one truth above all others that you and I crave after? It is not the assurance that no hurt or harm will come to us on this earthly pilgrimage. It is not the promise that nature will be gentle and benevolent. It is not even that we may be fully released men and women, the masters of our fate and the captains of our souls. The deepest, most passionate longing in the human soul is to know that God is and that God is good. That is the Truth above all others. Tell us that Love is on the throne of this Universe and that a heavenly Father has us in His keeping, and which one of us would not be prepared to go through hell itself, if we knew that at last we would find ourselves safe within our Father's door?

"I am the Truth," said Jesus. "If ye had known me, ye should have known my Father also". "No man cometh unto the Father but by me".[1] Have we known this Jesus, you and I? Have we believed in Him, trusted Him, and cast our care upon Him? No living soul can do that and not find the Father. No living soul can do that and not see God in the face of Jesus Christ. And that face is the face of Love, the answer to all our heart's yearnings, the cure of all our ills, the rest of all our souls and the assurance of all our safety. "Let not your heart be troubled . . . I am the true and living way . . . He that hath seen me hath seen the Father." Take another look at Jesus Christ and go in peace!

[1] St. John 14:6-7.